A Funny Thing
Happened . . .

A Funny Thing Happened . . .

Conservative Anecdotes
collected by
The Rt Hon Sir John Cope MP

with a foreword by
The Rt Hon Christopher Patten MP

Colt Books Ltd
Cambridge
in association with
Conservative Central Office

Colt Books Ltd
9 Clarendon Road
Cambridge CB2 2BH

in association with

Conservative Central Office,
32 Smith Square,
London SW1P 3HH

First published 1991

Drawings and jacket illustration by Philip Spence
Designed by Susie Home

British Library Cataloguing in Publication Data
   A funny thing happened: Conservative anecdotes.
   I. Cope, *Sir*, John
   828.02

   ISBN 0 905899 04 0

Printed and bound in Great Britain by Biddles Ltd, Guildford and Kings Lynn

Contents

Acknowledgements   7

Foreword by the Rt Hon Christopher Patten MP   9

Tory Stories   13

When in Rome   31

Down in the Constituency   43

The Dignity of Office   58

Mother of Parliaments   68

Canvassing Blues   84

Elections – The Acid Test   101

List of Contributors   125

Acknowledgements

I should like to thank Keith Reid for the original idea for this publication; the Conservative Research Department, particularly Martin Graham, for turning an idea into a project; and Linda Yeatman of Colt Books Ltd for turning a project into a book. My thanks are due, most of all, to the ranks of my Conservative colleagues in Westminster – past and present – for giving us all the benefit of some of their prized moments.

Long may politics continue to provide us with laughs – ensuring, not least, that we do not take ourselves *too* seriously!

The Rt Hon Sir John Cope MP
Deputy Chairman of the Conservative Party

Foreword

It would be hard to find a career with such exaggerated swings of fortune as politics. Up one minute. Down with a bump the next. No doubt it is good for the soul but it can be a bit trying on the nerves. There is nothing better than a good laugh over an anecdote to keep one sane in the darker moments.

In one of my earliest campaigns my Agent canvassed a house on behalf of a local councillor. When he asked the man whether the councillor could count on his support he received the reply: "I can't think why I should. He's just run off with my wife."

Anecdotes tend to accumulate as one becomes better known publicly. I remember travelling on a cross-channel ferry once. I noticed a couple nearby staring at me and nudging one another. After a bit of hesitation the man came up to me and said, "You must get pretty fed up with people saying this to you."

"Saying what?" I countered nervously.

"How like Chris Patten you look," he replied.

It would have been cruel to put him right!

Mind you, it's given me a new form of defence. The other day a taxi driver stopped his cab to give me some forthright advice on the state of the nation. I was able to reply that I couldn't understand why everyone mistook me for the Chairman of the Conservative Party!

I warmly recommend this book of anecdotes. I very much hope that it will bring a bit of sparkle into otherwise flat after-dinner speeches all over the country. If it can reduce the length of longueurs and raise a few hearty laughs instead, it will have done us all a good service. Happy reading.

The Rt Hon Christopher Patten MP
Chairman of the Conservative Party

Tory Stories

Robert Adley MP

Member for Christchurch

In 1975 I invited Margaret Thatcher to come to my constituency to speak. She became Prime Minister.

In 1990 I invited John Major to come to my constituency to speak. He became Prime Minister.

I am now available for aspiring opportunitists to approach me for a speaking engagement in 2005!

The Rt Hon Michael Howard MP

Member for Folkestone and Hythe, Secretary of State for Employment

A Conservative Member of Parliament was making his way to the House of Commons when he saw, on the other side of the road, a person lying on the footpath. He crossed to discover that the person had obviously been beaten up and was in need of medical attention. "Just hold on a moment," he said, "I shall go and ring for an ambulance."

Shortly afterwards, a Labour of Member of Parliament came along. He too crossed the road, looked at the person lying on the pavement and said, "Good Heavens! The person who did this to you really needs help. If only I knew who it was!"

The third person to pass by was a Liberal. On seeing the person lying on the footpath, he too crossed the road. He stooped low over the prostrate figure. "Tell me," he asked, "what did the others say?"

Peter Viggers MP

Member for Gosport
(Parliamentary Under-Secretary of State, Northern Ireland 1986-89)

A couple who are constituents of mine received a letter from their young daughter who was reaching the end of her first year at college. The letter read:

294b Station Road
Hackney

Dear Mummy and Daddy,

As you will see from the address, I am no longer living in College. The flat here is not too bad. There is only one bedroom but it is quite a good size and we also have a good amount of light and air considering it is a basement.

As to the people I am living with, Hank is pleasant enough. I have never found him violent – I think the police must provoke him. Abdul is *very* friendly; he says we will make lots of money from the plants he is growing on the windowsill.

You must not worry about me. I feel quite well each day after the morning sickness passes.

Your loving daughter,
Susan

PTO

the other side read:

Dear Mummy and Daddy,

Nothing I have written on the other side is true. I am still living at college and life is very pleasant. I am not pregnant and indeed I am playing for the College hockey team.

However, I do have to tell you that I have failed my first year's English exams. This is bad news . . . but I hope this letter will help you to keep it in perspective.

Your loving daughter,
Susan

Sir Anthony Kershaw
(MP *for Stroud* 1955-1987)

During the 1940s, a former Chairman of the National Union was asked to deputise as a speaker for Winston Churchill. He started his speech, "I am sorry you have been disappointed by Mr Churchill not being able to come. I am, as a matter of fact, surprised at being asked to stand in for him. I suppose it is because I have been a member of the Conservative Party for longer than Mr Churchill – though not of course so often."

The Lord Kimball

(MP *for Gainsborough* 1956-83)

I shall never forget hunting on Tuesday, 27th March 1979, before the vote which on Wednesday 28th finished the Socialist government.

We had a very good hunt on the last day to finish the season. Unfortunately, I took a wrong turn and got behind in the field. Approaching the road, full of the car followers, I heard the hunt terrier man saying at the top of his voice, "Where the hell is Marcus? I hope he hasn't fallen off and hurt himself, because we've jolly well got to get him to Westminster tomorrow night to finish off that lot."

The Rt Hon Sir Wyn Roberts MP

Member for Conwy, Minister of State, Welsh Office

I heard this definition of a European heaven and hell from a German Minister of Tourism in Berlin.

"Heaven is where the English do the politics, the French do the cooking, the Italians do the loving and the Germans do the organising."

"Hell is where the English do the cooking, the French do the politics, the Germans do the loving and the Italians do the organising."

There is an American version, of course.

"Heaven is an English home with a Japanese wife, Chinese cooking and an American salary."

"Hell is a Japanese home with English cooking, Chinese salary and an American wife."

John Watson

(MP for Skipton and Ripon 1979-1987)

I ran in the London Marathon in 1986. My time was four and a half hours.

The headline in my local paper read:

"MP completed Marathon – misses world record by two hours twenty minutes."

Elizabeth Peacock MP

Member for Batley and Spen

A constituent recently sent me this story:
A man lived by the side of the road and sold hot dogs. He was hard of hearing so he had no radio. He had trouble with his eyes so he never read newspapers nor watched television. But he sold good hot dogs.

He put up a sign telling how good they were. He stood at the side of the road and cried, "Buy a hot dog, Mister." And people bought.

He increased his meat and bun orders. He bought a bigger stove to take care of his trade. He got his son home from college to help him.

But then something happened . . . .

His son said, "Father, haven't you heard the news? There's a big recession on. The unemployment situation is terrible. The energy situation is worse."

Whereupon, the father thought, "Well, my son has been to college, he reads the newspapers and watches television and he ought to know."

So his father cut down on his meat and bun order, took down his sign and no longer bothered to stand on the highway to sell hot dogs. And his hot dog sales fell almost overnight.

"You're right, son," the father said. "We are certainly in the middle of a great recession."

Greg Knight MP

Member for Derby North, Lord Commissioner

The trouble with left-wingers is they can never admit when they are wrong. I like the story of a left-wing delegate attending a Labour Party conference who, seeing someone across a crowded committee room, hurried over and said, "Well, well, well, you have changed, Bill. You've lost a lot of weight, and your hair has gone all grey. I see you don't wear glasses any more and you've shaved off your beard. Bill Potts – I never thought the image makers at Walworth Road would get to you!"

The man replied, "But my name isn't Bill Potts – I'm Damien Waterhouse."

"Amazing," the left-winger replied, "you've even changed your name."

The Rt Hon Cecil Parkinson MP

Member for Hertsmere
(Chairman of the Conservative Party 1981-83, Secretary of State for Transport 1989-90)

Shortly after I became a Member of Parliament in 1970, I was asked to stand in for a ministerial speaker who could not keep a speaking engagement at an Area Women's conference. There were about three hundred women present and the only person in the room who was more nervous than I, was the Chairman.

After a long pause, she finally got up and started to introduce me. Her opening words were, "And now, ladies, I am going to give you Mr Parkinson's biological details."

She is still trying to work out why the audience laughed and I blushed.

The Rt Hon the Lord Boyd-Carpenter

(MP for Kingston upon Thames 1945-72, Chief Secretary to the Treasury 1962-64)

When my father, the late Sir Archibald Boyd-Carpenter, was MP for Coventry, I represented him at a meeting addressed by the Member of an adjoining constituency, Captain Hope.

The vote of thanks was made by a worthy local councillor, who spoke at great length and concluded with the words: "You will not want a long and dull speech from me after what you have heard from Captain Hope."

Sir Tom Normanton

(MP for Cheadle, 1970-1987, MEP for Cheshire East 1973-1989)

Before I entered the House, in 1970, I campaigned furiously against the squandermania of Socialist Government committed to high public spending and high taxation of our people. Imagine my joy when I happened to read the wise saying for the day on a one day, one slip, tear-off calendar:

> The halcyon days of parliamentary government were those when the Chancellor of the Exchequer lived within his income and without mine.

This provided a useful and flexible text around which to weave my passionate belief in Conservative fiscal principles.

One evening, I was invited to address a gathering of businessmen and responsible local and national civil servants, in non-party political terms of course. As I sat down, I noted to my horror my own Inspector of Taxes in the second row. When it came to studying my tax returns he often reminded my about that evening. "Are you sure that you have included all your income in this return to the Chancellor?"

Was it good humour on his part or a suspicious mind? I wonder!

John Lee MP
Member for Pendle

J ohn Lee, now Member of Parliament for Pendle, cut his political teeth fighting the safe Labour seat of Manchester Moss Side in the October 1974 General Election.

One Saturday evening, at the local Polish Club dance, he returned to the 'elders' table, after having danced with a particularly attractive blonde Polish girl, but observed that the 'elders' were clearly agitated and upset. He asked them why.

"Because the girl you've been dancing with is a prostitute. Your reputation is ruined – no votes for you here!"

J ohn Lee then moved on to politically greener pastures and in 1975 went before the selection committee in Nelson and Colne for the chance to fight the sitting Labour MP, Doug Hoyle.

One of his opponents for the candidacy was a young barrister from the south who faced questioning from a Conservative Association officer with a strong Lancashire accent.

"What's tha gonna do 'bout Doug 'oyle ?"

The barrister nervously fingered his tie and said: "I . . . I wasn't aware that there was any oil in this constituency!" (Barrister not chosen as Parliamentary candidate!)

Nicholas Baker MP

Member for North Dorset, Lord Commissioner

Car Chase

This story was recounted to me by a friend who had been to a dinner party in Hampstead.

After the dinner party had ended the hosts were in their kitchen washing the dishes and clearing away the dinner party debris. They turned on the wireless and happened to tune into the police network. After a series of messages it became apparent that a stolen car had been spotted by one police car which was calling on others for assistance. Rapidly, other cars were called in over the network and a hue and cry ensued. It seemed as if six or seven cars joined in what was becoming an exciting real-life drama as the stolen car bolted desperately this way and that to avoid the police car closing in.

The couple followed the chase with mounting excitement. Finally, the stolen car was reportedly trapped down a cul-de-sac and, to the surprise of the pursuing police cars and the amazement of the couple, enjoying the drama that was much more exciting than any television car chase, the stolen car disappeared at the end of the cul-de-sac and fell into the Regent's Park Canal.

Soon afterwards, the police hauled the stolen car out of the canal and gave over the network the stolen car's registration number. The couple recognised it – it was their own car! In horror, they ran to the kitchen window to see if their car was at it's accustomed parking place.

It had gone.

David Porter MP

Member for Waveney

Every year Margaret Thatcher held several receptions at 10 Downing Street for, among others, MPs and spouses. It was at a summer reception just a year after I was elected that she spent several minutes talking to my wife and me, which was much appreciated. She had by then already been Prime Minister and a world statesman for eight years. I was just one more back-bencher.

Sarah was quite obviously pregnant, so Mrs Thatcher asked about that, what were we hoping for, and about our other children, Victoria, Thomas and Samuel.

Some months later, we were awaiting Alice's birth, any day. The Prime Minister was walking down the Library Corridor in the Commons, surrounded by her entourage of Parliamentary Private Secretary, security man and a secretary when she passed me.

She stopped and turned back, the entourage swivelling too, to look at me. "And what did your wife have after all?" she asked.

I was impressed and honoured beyond measure.

The Rt Hon John Wakeham MP

Member for Colchester South and Maldon, Secretary of State for Energy

They say that "once bitten, twice shy".
Many years ago I was asked to pen two amusing jokes for a collection of stories in aid of a very worthy project. As any true politician would, I decided to keep the best jokes to myself and not make them available to all and sundry. So I recounted two of the worst jokes I knew – jokes which never raised a laugh when I told them.

A number of years later, I attended a very grand dinner and the host began his speech of introduction with those very same jokes I had contributed to the book. But, to my horror, instead of the stony silence I had always received in telling them, his audience erupted into howls of laughter.

From that moment on, I decided that discretion is the better part of valour and to keep *every* joke for my own use.

John Watson

(MP *for Skipton and Ripon 1979-1987*)

The Castelford Nuclear Fall-out Shelter, built to withstand a 35 megaton nuclear blast, was destroyed by vandals on the night of the cup final.

Greg Knight MP

Member for Derby North, Lord Commissioner

An MP who sent his only son to a private school was irritated when they doubled their fees due to 'increased overheads'. On examining their account notifying him of the increase, he observed a spelling mistake, the bill referring to fees due of £5,000 'per anum'.

The MP returned their account, with a note that he would "prefer as before, to pay through the nose".

Lord Elliott of Morpeth

(MP *for Newcastle upon Tyne 1957-83*)

An Association AGM

Some years ago, accompanied by John Lacy, at that time our Central Office Agent, Northern Area, I attended as guest speaker the AGM of one of our County Durham Associations.

The platform party was assembled in a room at the back of the hall. To the obvious irritation of the President, the Chairman had not arrived. Eventually it was decided that we would start without him, and we duly marched down the central aisle to the platform. The business part of the meeting was over and I had begun to speak, when the double doors at the back opened, and the Chairman (who had been re-elected in his absence) appeared. He proceeded a little unsteadily toward the platform, smiling benignly and nodding right and left as he came. I continued with my speech and the dialogue then went as follows:

SELF:	It is important that all members of our Party are at this time steadfast in support of the leadership . . .
PRESIDENT:	Where have you been?
CHAIRMAN:	You should have waited.
SELF:	Our policies are sound, and based on superior experience . . .
PRESIDENT:	You're drunk!
CHAIRMAN:	I'm not – shut up!
SELF:	I now turn to the all important balance of payments position . . .
PRESIDENT:	You're a disgrace – you're disgusting.
CHAIRMAN:	Shut up, you old bastard.

SELF: This leads me into the continuing problems for our region . . .

PRESIDENT: Angry growling.

CHAIRMAN: I'm fed up with your carping criticism.

WOMEN'S CHAIRMAN: Stop it you two!

SELF: Unemployment sadly continues to be of major concern . . .

PRESIDENT: I'm not sitting here any longer listening to your drunken remarks.

CHAIRMAN: Please your bloody self!

SELF: As I have often stated, our region is capable of making a major contribution to national prosperity . . .

At this point the President left the platform, strode down the central aisle and banged the double doors as he left.

CHAIRMAN: Rude b . . . .

SELF: Above all, I also welcome this opportunity to thank you for your constant support of the Party – here where the going is far from easy.

CHAIRMAN: Hear hear!

The meeting over, the Chairman entertained John and me to a splendid dinner in a nearby hotel. He didn't actually have any food himself, explaining that he had something on the train which had been delayed – the reason for his late arrival.

Nicholas Winterton MP

Member for Macclesfield

People sometimes ask what is a Member of Parliament worth, and in response I tell them of my experience. When I was sitting down to breakfast at The Elgin, a comfortable family hotel in Blackpool, on the second day of the Conservative Party Conference in 1981, I was brought, by a member of staff of the hotel, a letter from my solicitor. The letter contained the information that I was being sued by John DeLorean for comments that I had made about his operations for $250 million (at that time £133m). It was, to say the least, a very interesting start to the day and I wonder whether any other back-bench Member of Parliament has been valued so highly.

I am glad to say that Mr DeLorean's case was struck out by a Master in the High Court and I was awarded a modest sum as a result of my counter-action for defamation. But I never received a penny. Mr DeLorean and his company sometime thereafter went into receivership.

An entertaining but very sobering experience.

Tony Baldry MP

Member for Banbury, Parliamentary Under-Secretary of State, Department of the Environment

In the February 1974 General Election, I was personal aide to Maurice Macmillan. At the start of the campaign, Maurice was suffering from a heavy attack of bronchitis. It was difficult discussing his adoption meeting speech with him as he was in bed, heavily medicated and without his false teeth! However, we managed and all was well.

In the October 1974 General Election, I volunteered to be personal aide to Margaret Thatcher. I was interviewed by her then personal secretary, Alison Ward (now Mrs John Wakeham) who wanted to know if I knew what was involved in being a PA. I recounted my experience with Maurice Macmillan to demonstrate that so far as I was concerned being a PA involved mucking in and doing whatever was required.

On hearing this story, Alison retorted: "Well, Mrs Thatcher writes all her own speeches. She doesn't wear false teeth and I don't suppose you will be seeing very much of her in bed!"

The Rt Hon the Lord Hailsham of St Marylebone KG CH

(MP for Oxford City 1938-50, St Marylebone 1963-70, Chairman of the Conservative Party 1957-59, Lord Chancellor 1979-87)

I was sitting on the top of a mountain in central Switzerland, called the Grosse Mythen, in the company of my brother Neil Hogg and an old Swiss guide, since sadly deceased. We were eating sandwiches.

Up comes a total stranger, a young man, and accosts me. The following conversation took place:

TS: "Are you who I think you are?

QH: "How am I to know who you think I am?"

TS: "Are you not Lord Butler?"

QH: "No, as a matter of fact, I am not Lord Butler."

TS: (in great confusion and blushing scarlet): "I am so sorry. I thought you were an English politician."

End of conversation. Collapse of all parties.

Edwina Currie MP

Member for Derbyshire South
(Under-Secretary of State for Health 1986-88)

I love graffiti. How about these, seen out canvassing in and around Derby:

"BRITISH RAIL ADVISE
THAT THIS RIGHT OF WAY
IS NOT DEDICATED TO THE PUBLIC."

Underneath: *"Neither is British Rail."*

Poster for a national newspaper series:

"HOW LABOUR WILL WIN"

Underneath:
"Next week: How to nail jelly to the ceiling"

When in Rome

The Rt Hon the Lord Barber

(MP for Doncaster 1951-64, Altrincham and Sale 1965-74, Chairman of the Conservative Party 1967-70, Chancellor of the Exchequer 1970-74)

When I accompanied Harold Macmillan on his first visit to the Soviet Union, he asked me to find out what he might say in Russian to those who turned out to greet him. The advice of our Foreign Office interpreter was that he could say, "DOBRYE DYEN" – pronounced DOBRAJIN – which means "GOOD DAY". I duly passed this on to Harold, who carefully and accurately practised it several times.

When we arrived at the next engagement there was quite a crowd. He now knew exactly what to say and he repeated his greeting with consistent success wherever we went from Leningrad to the Ukraine. He waved to the crowd and called out in a loud voice: "DOUBLE GIN, DOUBLE GIN." The response was immediate. They cheered and clapped.

David Mudd MP

Member for Falmouth and Cambourne

The guide had been tolerant. As a graduate of the People's Republic of China guides' charm school, he had learned to tolerate the incredulity of western tourists to the wilder excesses of his enthusiasm for life in modern China.

The great day came – the obligatory visit to the birthplace of Doctor Sun Yat-Sen, founder of the revolution and patron saint of tourism in Guanzhou.

"We apploach birthplace of Sun Yat-Sen," he announced with pride. "Sun Yat-Sen not like other childlen. While they play, he study. While they lead books, he consider impact of capitalism on poor people. While other boys and girls play clicket, he make and learn to thlow hand glenades.

"He was, as you impelialists say, a light broody plat."

Peter Temple-Morris MP
Member for Leominster

The Perils of Foreign Travel

In Washington for the inauguration of President Reagan's second term, January 1985, salubrious hotel, 3 am, problems in getting breakfast order onto outside door knob of room. Stepped out too far. Door slammed shut. Standing there in full glory of underpants and absolutely nothing else. What does one do? How to protect British Parliamentary dignity abroad? Oh My God, the tabloids!

To utter horror, a woman rounded the bend of the corridor. In the finest of American intrepid tradition she marched by me as if I wasn't there. Agonizing wait. Man arrived, loan of mackintosh and arrival of night porter. As I grovelled an apology, the porter got me back into the room

with the gently drawled comment, "Don't worry, Sir. It happens all the time."

Wonderful place the USA!

The Rt Hon Ian Lang MP

Member for Galloway and Upper Nithsdale, Secretary of State for Scotland

As Industry Minister I was due to take part in a Scottish trade mission to Japan. But parliamentary business got slightly in the way . . . .

It was a glorious sunny day as I arrived at Heathrow mid-morning on October 30, 1990. The British Airways noon flight BA 017 for Moscow and Tokyo took off on time.

At Sheremetievo Airport, Moscow, we got out to stretch our legs.

Just as we were boarding the plane again, a British Airways official told us that there was an urgent message for us to ring London. But – he added helpfully – there was no telephone and no time, so there was nothing we could do about it!

As we crossed the Ural mountains, we concluded that although the message could have been about almost anything, the most likely news was that we were to turn back because the Government was in a mess over voting on the dog registration scheme.

With the pilot's help, we made radio contact with the Secretary of State's office in London. Yes, it *was* dogs, and yes, I was to come back at once. A further call to the Whip's office to negotiate – after all, they had cleared us to go to Japan – but yes, it was imperative that I get back to Westminster in time for a vote at 6 pm the next day. All Ministers, they added helpfully, from all over the world, were being summoned home.

We were over the Central Siberian Plateau at the time, and about half way to our 6,000-mile destination. "You do realise," said Ken Thomson, playing our last card, "that he's in Siberia at the moment?"

"Well tell him to get the hell out of Siberia," came the reply.

It was a glorious sunny day as I arrived at Narita Airport, Tokyo, in mid-morning on October 31. Mr Humfrey from The Embassy greeted me with the helpful news that I was booked on a flight for London two hours later.

We just had time to discuss how best to salvage our Japanese programme before I boarded the 1.40 pm flight to

Heathrow, and settled down to watch "Back to the Future 3" – again.

I arrived at Heathrow just before 6 pm and was rushed off the plane in the hope I would still be in time for the crucial vote. As I came through customs, I met Graeme Herbert. "Bad news," said Graeme. "The vote is off – the House of Lords defeated the dog registration scheme by nineteen votes. You are not needed after all."

It was a glorious sunny day as I arrived at Heathrow midmorning on November 1 . . .

Dame Janet Fookes DBE MP
Member for Plymouth Drake

Tell It To The Marines

I was thrilled to be included in the VIP week organised by the Royal Marines during their period of Arctic Training in Norway, but was not best pleased to find that one highlight of the visit – a night out in a tent in the Arctic – was crossed out in my case and an hotel substituted. All my feminist hackles rose as I enquired why I should be thus discriminated against! Diligent enquiries revealed that it was worry about the provision of outside loos that was causing concern, upon which I declared firmly that if I didn't find it embarrassing neither should they.

It was certainly the coldest and most uncomfortable night that I had ever spent anywhere. I was provided with warm moonboots, a cosy sleeping bag and a hot supper from the hands of no less a person than a General in the Royal Marines. None of these sufficed to keep out the cold, and the ground felt harder by the hour. Never have I had so many men lying at my feet and yet ironically all I had to hug were my outdoor boots. These have to be kept inside the sleeping bag, or they are frozen stiff by the morning and impossible to get on.

It was certainly a night to remember, but not for any romantic reasons!

Sir Robert Rhodes James MP
Member for Cambridge

As a founder-member of the Anglo-Hungarian Round Table, with Giles Radice, one of the high points of our visit to Hungary in 1978 was to a collective farm. We had already discovered how excellent Hungarian wine can be, and there was plenty on offer at dinner. Afterwards, the head of the collective tottered to his feet to deliver the most brilliantly subversive speech I had ever heard in a Communist country.

He opened with the words, "Since Communism came to Hungary we have had more swine than ever before!" and it went on from there. It went down very well indeed, but there were some stony faces as well. I have often wondered what happened to him. I hope he prospers in the Free Hungary.

Tony Baldry MP

Member for Banbury, Parliamentary Under-Secretary of State, Department of the Environment

Off to the Moon

I was fortunate enough to be a member of the inter-Parliamentary Union delegation led by Lord Whitelaw, that went to the Soviet Union shortly after Gorbachev had become their head of government.

Everyone in Moscow treated Lord Whitelaw with a very considerable degree of respect and no little awe. But in due course, the reason for this became a little clearer. *Pravda* had interpreted Lord Whitelaw's official title of Lord President of the Privy Council into Lord President of the Secret Council. Muscovites were evidently under the impression that Willie Whitelaw was the UK equivalent of the head of the KGB!

In due course, the delegation visited Star City where the Russians train potential cosmonauts. Shortly after we arrived, the officials organising the visit ceremoniously presented Willie Whitelaw with a medal. Lord Whitelaw enquired what this medal was for. It was always given to cosmonauts, he was told, immediately before they went off into space!

John Lacy

General Director of Party Campaigning, Conservative Central Office

At the Jamaican General Election in 1989, I was advisor to the Jamaican Labour Party, which is the Conservative Party in Jamaica!

The JLP, led by Eddie Seaga, was being challenged by the Socialist PNP, led by Michael Manley.

The influence of the Jamaican singer, Bob Marley, on the campaign meant that both parties had flagship songs with all-embracing themes played throughout the twenty-five day campaign.

The PNP (Socialist Party) lyrics were:

> *The PNP ready, ready to serve Jamaica.*
> *We tired of the poverty and hunger,*
> *We sick and tired of the heap a false promises,*
> *We sick and tired of the high prices.*
> *The Seaga government is a pain,*
> *Many millions gone down the drain,*
> *So mek we vote dem out, come mek we vote dem out.*

The JLP (Conservative Party) jingle had an infectious rhythm along with a great release of energy and praised Eddie Seaga for what he had done as Prime Minister:

> *No food pan the shelf, Eddie put it back,*
> *No money inna yu pocket, a Eddie put it back,*
> *No light pan the street, a Eddie put it back,*
> *No clothes pan yu back, a Eddie put it back.*
> *Spread out, spread out all Labourites,*
> *Come we spread out.*

There is no justice – Eddie Seaga lost!

Sir Thomas Arnold MP

Member for Hazel Grove, Vice Chairman of the Conservative Party

During the course of a long, private journey through Southern Africa in the summer of 1978, I was summoned to pay a courtesy call upon His Excellency The Life President of Malawi, Dr Banda. I was accompanied by Mr John Gardiner (currently the Private Secretary to the Chairman of the Conservative Party), Mrs Gwenneth Knight (a US citizen), Miss Verena Spillmann (Swiss), Miss Sylvia Huri (Egyptian) and Miss Penelope Eastwood (now Lady Romsey).

After greeting Mr Gardiner and myself, Dr Banda turned to Mrs Knight and asked, "And where is your constituency?"

"Cambridge, Massachusetts!" she replied in a nasal twang.

"Miss Spillmann?"

"Solothurn, Switzerland!"

"Miss Huri?"

"Alexandria, Egypt!"

"Miss Eastwood?"

"Palma, Majorca!"

"My, my," said His Excellency the Life President. "This is the strangest – but, certainly the most attractive – British Parliamentary Delegation to grace this Palace. You are most welcome!"

Christine Wall

Head of News, Conservative Central Office

It was my first foreign trip as a press officer at No 10. I had been in the job about six weeks when Bernard Ingham called me in and told me I would be looking after the media on a trip to Washington.

All went well until shortly before the return flight home, when we were informed that we would be delayed for

twelve hours because of fog. The media had checked out of their hotel, had nothing to do and were growing increasingly impatient. Realising I was but seconds away from an outbreak of severe media mutiny, I set about trying to be as helpful as possible.

I managed to take care of their luggage and hire a mini-bus to take them on a sight-seeing tour to wherever they wished. A vote was taken and the Smithsonian Institute was decided upon. I duly bundled all my charges into the bus, stood on the hotel steps and waved them goodbye.

Feeling rather pleased that I had managed the situation well, I returned to my room where the phone was ringing.

"Look, it's Bernard here. I'm with the Prime Minister. As we've been delayed, she has decided to make a completely private visit to the Smithsonian Institute, so for goodness sake don't let on to the press . . . ."

The Rt Hon David Howell MP

Member for Guildford
(Secretary of State for Transport 1981-83)

No Breakfast with Mrs Thatcher

The scene is the G-7 Summit meeting in Venice, summer 1980. I am accompanying the Prime Minister as Energy Secretary, along with Peter Carrington and Geoffrey Howe.

First briefing meetings of the day are scheduled at 8.15 am. But that is not early enough for Mrs Thatcher. The Prime Ministerial party is ordered to parade at 6 am to visit some frescoes in a church on a distant Venetian island and, hopefully, to have breakfast there.

41

Bleary-eyed, we stagger down at dawn to the waiting motor-launches. Soon, the fresh lagoon wind blowing on our faces is replacing sleepiness with pangs of hunger.

The island is reached and there, under an awning – blissful sight – a lavish breakfast is laid out on white tablecloths, with the smell of fresh coffee on the breeze.

But the Prime Minister sweeps us by. The purpose is not eating but viewing frescoes.

What is more, these turn out to be frescoes being restored high up the church walls and only visible if one climbs six storeys of scaffolding platforms, connected by ladders. Would we now all like to start climbing?

Most of the party, now faint from hunger, decline and start drifting out of the church towards those beckoning tables. Not so Mrs T.

In a trice, she is six floors up bombarding the experts with questions. It turns out that the scientific techniques required to restore these paintings are unusual. More experts are called, more questions asked.

The Prime Minister descends and explains the technical points to the feebler members of her party.

By now, time is pressing. Officials are anxiously looking at their watches. The motor boats are revving up and we are herded back in.

There is no time for breakfast.

What a frivolous idea!

Down in the Constituency

The Rt Hon the Lord Jenkin of Roding

(MP for Wanstead and Woodford 1964-87, Secretary of State for the Environment 1983-85)

S hortly after the 1970 Election, my small son's bicycle went missing. I told him to report it to the local police, where the conversation went thus:

SMALL BOY: "Please sir, I think my bike has been pinched."

LARGE POLICEMAN BEHIND DESK: "Very sorry to hear that, my son; perhaps we had better start with your address."

Small boy gives policeman our home address.

POLICEMAN: "Oooooh! Financial Secretary to the Treasury, eh?"

SMALL BOY (BREATHLESSLY): "Oh no, sir! That's my father!"

Note: small boy is now prospective Conservative candidate for Colchester North!

The Hon Timothy Sainsbury MP

Member for Hove, Minister for Trade

Brighton and Hove Albion's ground is The Goldstone, which is in Hove. The Club has spent most of its history as a 2nd or 3rd Division side. In 1983, they were in the 1st Division and to general astonishment reached the Cup Final, which was played against Manchester United, during the Election Campaign.

Against all expectations, the Wembley match was an exciting 2-2 draw. The whole event, not surprisingly, aroused great enthusiasm in Hove and the Club colours, blue and white, were displayed throughout the town on cars and shop windows, on rosettes and banners.

This led the Labour candidate to suggest that the Election should be postponed as this widespread display of blue and white gave a misleading idea of the political sympathies of the town.

As Conservative candidate, I asked: "What about Manchester United? After all, they play in red."

Sadly, Manchester United won the replay. But the Conservatives won the seat, and Labour finished third!

John Watson

(MP *for Skipton and Ripon* 1979-87)

A lady came to my surgery with her dog to complain about a report that the dog licence was going up from 37p to £5. That, she said, was more than the rate of inflation. She was right. It was.

"Well," I said, "it might not be £5 in your case because your dog's only black and white."

This was a joke. But it was not recognised as such. So I said I was joking.

"It may be a joke to you, Mr Watson, but me and Nathan take it very seriously indeed," she replied.

At the next election she had a Labour poster in the window.

Sir William van Straubenzee
(MP *for Wokingham* 1959-87)

I have always attached the very greatest importance to being out and about in my constituency. One startled constituent, shortly after I was first elected in 1959, looked at me with astonishment and said, "Gor blimey, I've never seen a live one before."

I also attached importance to sending birthday cards to those who became eighteen. In my case they were always signed personally. Many is the time subsequently when I have met people who had received such cards. I was once approached by a charming lady who said what pleasure the birthday card had given to her son, whom we will call Alfie, but she pulled my leg that I had sent it to him a year too early.

I was about to reply, "That, Madam, is because you filled in the form incorrectly," when she told me Alfie's story. A week or so before his eighteenth birthday, Alfie had gone into his local pub for a drink. Recognized by the landlord, he was sent out with his tail between his legs for not being eighteen. Shortly afterwards, he re-entered the pub triumphantly brandishing the birthday card which had been sent to him a year too early, saying, "There you are, the MP says I am eighteen."

45

He got his drink. I hope he remained a faithful Conservative ever after.

The Rt Hon the Lord Fraser of Carmyllie

The Lord Advocate
(MP *for Angus South* 1979-83, *Angus East* 1983-87)

At the height of Marathon mania, I was invited to make a speech and fire the pistol to set off the 1983 Dundee Marathon. Much against her better judgement my wife had been persuaded to join in the run.

As she stood pale amidst the milling competitors, the organisers told me to cut my speech to the bare minimum to ensure the race began on time. All I had time for was:

"It is my duty to start this Marathon and my wife's duty to finish it."

A constituent approached me, saying, "That's the only decent speech you've ever made. It was short and for once it had a point!"

James Pawsey MP

Member for Rugby and Kenilworth

To understand my anecdote you should remember that I am the father of six sons.

Shortly after I was elected in 1979, I visited a primary school in my constituency and was introduced to the

Reception Class as Rugby's new MP. The head teacher asked if anyone could say what MP stands for, and a little boy put up his hand and said it stood for 'Military Police'! After some shuffling of feet another said it stood for 'Missing Persons'. After a good deal more shuffling of feet a little girl who lives in the next village and knows our family well said, "No Miss, MP stands for More Pawseys."

Sir Dudley Smith MP
Member for Warwick and Leamington

This is a true story.
An old and valued colleague of mine retired at the last election after over twenty-five years of loyal service. He was extremely popular in his mainly rural seat and the local Association gave him a special farewell party in his largest village.

Before the bunfight in the village hall, which was packed, there were formal tributes from worthies so numerous that they had to sit in two lines on the platform. The ancient President insisted on presiding. He began by extolling the virtues of my former colleague and added, his voice breaking with emotion: "It is not too much to say that he was loved by many of us, and no more so than by dear old Freddie Frobisher." Mr Frobisher was a former President. Putting his hand to his brow, he looked out, searched the audience and added: "I can't see Freddie here, but I'm sure he will be with us in a minute. He wouldn't miss this evening for worlds."

This comment caused much murmuring in the audience. The Agent, sitting in the row immediately behind, tugged

47

the President's sleeve and whispered: "Freddie Frobisher died ten years ago." Unfortunately, the ancient President was very deaf. He turned back to the audience and said: "Ah ladies and gentlemen, I'm advised that dear old Freddie is with us after all."

Jonathan Sayeed MP

Member for Bristol East

On one occasion, I was driving up the motorway to Bristol early one Saturday. As I was late for my advice centre, the speed at which I was travelling caught the attention of a police car.

"Are you aware, Sir, of how fast you are driving?" asked the officer.

"I am sorry, officer, I'm afraid I am late for my surgery," was the unpremeditated reply.

"In that case," said the policeman magnaminously, "drive on. We can't keep all those sick people waiting, can we, doctor?"

Ian Taylor MP

Member for Esher

I was playing cricket for a team outside my constituency, which had no connection with politics. After scoring a few runs, I was hit in the face by an awkward bouncer, and retired bloody and hurt. I later returned to the crease only to be caught immediately in the field by the person who had earlier bowled at me. Before I went to the hospital, to be stitched up, the culprit admitted that he was one of my constituents.

A few weeks later at a village fete, a lady asked after my health and then admitted that she was the mother of the cricketer. She assured me that, regardless of how he had voted in the past, he and the rest of the family now felt obliged to turn out for me at the next election!

Howzat!

Hugo Summerson MP

Member for Walthamstow

A man from Walthamstow was out one evening walking his dog. A passing policeman noticed that he was carrying what looked like a large chisel.

"I need it for defence against werewolves," the man said.

The policeman arrested him, and he was duly charged with carrying an offensive weapon.

When the man appeared in court, he stated again that he always carried the chisel, when he walked his dog, for protection against werewolves. In the course of his evidence he repeated this explanation at least four times. The jury, obviously impressed, retired to consider their verdict. Then a note came out from the jury room to defence counsel. It read, "Are there any werewolves in this area?"

The Rt Hon John Biffen MP

Member for Shropshire North
(Leader of the House of Commons and Lord Privy Seal 1982-87)

The Hazards of Selection

The Oswestry constituency, now renamed North Shropshire, has always been my Parliamentary home, and I could not have been luckier in the accident of selection that made me the Member in 1961. It was rural heartland evoking memories of my upbringing. Shortly after selection, but before adoption for the Oswestry seat, certain rivals circulated the deadly rumour that I was a London journalist foisted upon the constituency by Conservative Central Office.

My parents were summoned from their Somerset farm to attend the adoption meeting. They were a living refutation of the slur. However, salvation brought its own danger; my father was such a 'natural' in the Oswestry Smithfield market that I heard farmers say they wished they had "the guv'nor and not the lad" as candidate.

Barry Field MP

Member for Isle of Wight

In the autumn of 1990, I received a letter from an island constituent which commenced with a paragraph some of which was in capitals and heavily underlined:

"Dear Mr Field,
What are you going to do about the disgusting state of Shanklin Pier . . ."

The day after the receipt of the letter, the hurricane came, the pier went.

My reputation as a Constituency Member of Parliament and a man of action has never looked back!

John Watson

(MP for Skipton and Ripon 1979-87)

I was invited to the AGM of the Pateley Bridge branch of my Conservative Association in 1985. It was December. I commented to the Chairman that December was an unusual month for an AGM. Most branches held them in October.

"We had it in October," he said, "but not enough people turned up. So we decided to have it tonight and to provide an incentive for people to come."

51

I said, "Oh, and I suppose I'm the incentive."
"No," he said, "we've got a meat pie."

Jonathan Sayeed MP

Member for Bristol East

Just after the 1983 General Election, I was doing a walkabout in Bristol East, which had long been a Labour stronghold held by Tony Benn.

A door in one of the streets was eventually opened by an elderly lady with thick pebble glasses and the intent look of one who is hard of hearing.

Speaking very loudly and clearly, I said: "Good morning, madam, I am your new Conservative Member of Parliament, Jonathan Sayeed." She surveyed me for a long moment, and then exclaimed: "Oh, Mr Benn, you don't look half as daft as they say!"

Sir Michael Marshall MP

Member for Arundel
(Parliamentary Under-Secretary of State, Department of Industry 1979-81)

My first ever constituency surgery got off to a bad start. Standing as the Conservative for Hartlepool against the Labour sitting member, I found, perhaps inevitably, that there was little response to my offer to help constituents.

However, one day I received a request for a meeting in the constituency office. My caller turned out to be one of those men who are sometimes described as a member of the 'dirty mac' brigade.

As his tales of sexual fantasy grew longer and longer, I decided that efficiency should rule over party pride. When my visitor paused for breath, I said, "I am so sorry to hear of your problems, but it is only fair to tell you that I am not yet a Member of Parliament. Have you considered going to see your existing Member of Parliament?"

"Oh yes. I have seen him several times and he sent me to see you."

Hugh Dykes MP

Member for Harrow East

A year or so ago, visiting yet another old peoples' home and having had a good week both in Parliament and in the Constituency, I was in an expansive mood and in what my wife describes as my 'slightly smarmy mode'. As the very charming lady – they used to be called Matrons, but are now called 'Executive Care Officers' and such like – was showing me round, we went into the television room where a large group of very nice, but very old, ladies was ensconced. Fortunately, it was after *Neighbours*, otherwise I would have been in trouble.

Leaning over one very ancient white-haired old dear, who peered up quizzically (she had cotton wool behind one lens of her extremely thick spectacles) with my wife looking alarmed that I was overdoing it, I boomed out in the best politician's 'glad handing', "Here is a wonderful dear old white-haired lady, let me say 'hello' to you."

As she peered up she uttered the immortal response, "B . . . . r off, you old sod. I'm Labour!"

Greg Knight MP

Member for Derby North, Lord Commissioner

Members of Parliament get all sorts of problems at their constituency surgeries. One young man who was doubtful over his matrimonial intentions went to see his MP to get some advice.

He unfolded his heart to his local Member and explained that he was not sure what he should do. He needed advice on whether he should marry a wealthy, but ugly old widow, who was chasing after him, or whether he should marry the pretty, but penniless young girl that he loved.

The MP had no hesitation in giving his opinion.

MP: "Listen to your heart, son, and take the advice it gives you. Marry the girl you love."

YOUNG MAN: "Yes. I think you are right. On reflection, that is what I ought to do. Thank you so very much for pointing me in the right direction. How can I ever repay you?"

MP: "Give me the old crow's address."

Lord Bethell MEP

Member for London North West

How Important is an MEP?

I recall the lady who telephoned me and said, "I live in Willesden and you are my Member of the European Parliament."

I said, "Yes."

She said, "There is a rat in my kitchen."

I replied, "In that case, I think you should immediately contact your Environmental Health Officer."

There was a pause. Then she said, "Well, thank you, but no. I don't think it is a matter that I ought to take to that high a level."

Allan Stewart MP

Member for Eastwood

The wife of an up and coming Conservative MP was entertaining his constituency office-bearers to dinner. Anxious to impress, she had prepared fresh salmon which was lying on the work surface beautifully cooked and decorated with cucumber, lemon and dill. Returning to the kitchen having helped her husband to greet their guests, she was horrified to find the cat making inroads into one end of the salmon.

Resourcefully, she chased the cat firmly out of the back door, turned the salmon over, re-arranged the garnish and transferred the delicious looking repast to the safety of the

dining room. Half an hour later and about to serve the meal, she opened the back door to put something in the dustbin and found the cat lying dead on the door mat!

Her panic was almost complete but, fortified by a stiff brandy from a handy decanter she made a courageous decision. In the drawing-room gin and tonics had done their work well and the party was going with a swing. Her slightly hysterical announcement that the cat had eaten the salmon and James would go down to the local chip shop to seek less elegant replacements was greeted with merriment and applause. The dinner was a huge success.

Imagine her chagrin the next morning to receive a call from her neighbour. "I'm terribly sorry about your cat, Elizabeth. Duncan found it hit by a car on the main road yesterday evening – he said it died instantly. We knew you had important guests for dinner and that's why he left it outside the back door."

The Dignity of Office

The Rt Hon Kenneth Baker MP

Member for Mole Valley, Home Secretary
(Chairman of the Conservative Party 1989-90)

One of my predecessors as Home Secretary wanted to
leave his mark. He asked his officials to consider what
initiatives he could take to improve the law and order of
our country. The officials suggested to him that it was time
for a crackdown on pornography. A series of measures was
duly worked up, in particular, one increasing the penalties
on pornographic videos.

He announced this great package, hoping it would secure
for him a niche in the Hall of Fame. It was generally well
received. But he had a cruel awakening the next day when
he opened *The Times* to discover the headline: "Home
Secretary to Act on Porn Videos."

The Rt Hon the Lord Havers

(MP for Wimbledon 1970-87, Lord Chancellor 1987)

It was during the Falklands War when the Prime Minister
invited me to Chequers to discuss the restricted zones
around the islands. We got down on our hands and knees
with the charts and agreed increases in the restricted
areas.

About an hour later Admiral Sir John Fieldhouse arrived and we went though the same procedure. When we finished, the Prime Minister invited us to have a drink and we sat in three high-backed chairs in her study, with her in the middle and the Admiral and I on each side.

The Admiral asked me if I had served in *HMS Norfolk* in the Far East during the war. He then asked me if I was the Signal Officer. Finally, he said that he was my Signal Midshipman.

The Prime Minister was looking from side to side as if she were at Wimbledon. She then asked, "Which of you is the senior?"

The Admiral said at once, "Oh, but the Attorney General, ma'am. I always called him 'sir'."

And my stock went up to the ceiling.

John Lee MP

Member for Pendle

In 1983, with four years in Parliament under his belt, John Lee was appointed Parliamentary Under-Secretary of State for Defence Procurement at the Ministry of Defence.

His daughters, Deborah aged seven and Elspeth aged six, were warned by their mother not to go into Daddy's Red Box.

"But Mummy," said Deborah, "we're only children and we're not going to tell the Germans the war secrets!"

While Defence Minister, John Lee was lobbied hard by the captain of the Army's famous free-fall parachute display team, the 'Red Devils' for a Government contribution of £150,000 towards a new aircraft for the team.

Finally, after a series of meetings, John Lee, a reluctant flier at the best of times, was offered a 'bribe'.

"Minister, if we get the £150,000 and are able to buy the new plane, *you* can be the first to jump!"

(Ministerial enthusiasm for the new aircraft rapidly waned!

Harry Greenway MP
Member for Ealing North

My uncle, Reginald Greenway, one of Her Majesty's Inspectors of Schools for thirty years, told of the visit of Sir Edward Boyle Bt MP to Doncaster Grammar School for Speech Day at a time when he was Minister for Education.

The chairman of the occasion was a Labour Mayor who 'did not seem to have done his homework'. When introducing the Minister, he read out a long list of biographical details ending with the peroration: "So ladies and gentleman, I give you the Minister for Education, Sir Edward Boyle, BTM – P."

The Rt Hon the Viscount Whitelaw
(MP *for Penrith and Borders* 1955-83, *Chairman of the Conservative Party* 1974-75, *Deputy Leader of the Conservative Party* 1975-91)

My Arrival in Northern Ireland

The day after I was appointed Secretary of State for Northern Ireland in 1972, we arrived at the airport to be met by the government representative with a copy of the *Belfast Newsletter*, the main Conservative paper. The headline read: PROMINENT ENGLISH ROMAN CATHOLIC APPOINTED AS SECRETARY OF STATE.

61

The government representative said to me, "If this is true, it is very serious. If it is not true, we must do something about it."

I replied, "Well, in fact I was brought up as a Scottish Presbyterian and I am now a member of the Church of England. Surely we can put that across."

The answer from the government representative: "You will learn in this place it is very much easier to put out a totally false statement than it is to contradict it."

I was to learn how true that was in the years immediately afterwards.

Iain Mills MP

Member for Meriden

As PPS to Norman Tebbit, who was then Secretary of State for Trade and Industry, I organised a visit to a small factory in Walsall, where about a hundred people were employed. After the main part of the visit, we entered what they called the finishing room.

There was a very distinguished, well-dressed gentleman doing a small task in the corner, and I asked him why he was doing it. He replied, "I am Director of Distribution, but in order to get the product despatched I am personally finishing off these goods."

I beckoned to the Secretary of State to come and hear this marvellous example of management involvement, when, behind him, the owner of the factory said, "He's doing it because he's my father."

Baroness Trumpington

Minister of State, Agriculture, Fisheries and Food

My first outside engagement after being appointed to MAFF, was to visit the South Sheep Show. Standing on a platform inside a marquee, the President of the Show introduced me to a large crowd with the following words:

"In life there are three things to avoid, an old dog, an old sheep and an old woman. Meet Lady Trumpington."

The Rt Hon Sir Peter Morrison MP

Member for City of Chester
(Deputy Chairman of the Conservative Party 1986-89)

I made a speech some years ago, at a Civil Service Headquarters seminar, entitled, *What I expect of Civil Servants,* in which I said:

"Some Civil Servants have certainly made themselves a laughing stock in terms of acronyms. I don't know whether you realise it, but they have a new committee called the Further Adult Training Programme Implementation Group, or FAT PIG. That is bad enough, but Miss Bacon is in the Chair!"

The Rt Hon Michael Jopling MP

Member for Westmoreland and Lonsdale.
(Minister of Agriculture, Fisheries and Food 1983-87)

S hould a former Whip tell anecdotes?
Sir Freddie Warren, the former Private Secretary to the Chief Whip, used to say: "Whipping, like stripping, should be done in private."

Donald Thompson MP

Member for Calder Valley
(Lord Commissioner of The Treasury 1983-86)

I was sent on a ministerial visit to some farms in one of the most beautiful parts of England. I was met by the local Ministry of Agriculture man and a Chairman of the National Union of Farmers. Before we set off on our tour of farms and food manufacturing, the NFU man said he'd see me at lunch with some of his friends and that they would cross examine me.

Off I went on my tour, eventually arriving at about half past twelve at an old farmhouse where I was greeted by the Chairman's wife. I was introduced to her sister and a couple of other ladies who were there to help with lunch. We got on famously which was just as well.

The time to eat arrived. Mushroom soup was served and it was perfect. My host, the Chairman of the NFU, produced two postcards and propped them against a wine bottle.

"Now then, Minister," he said, "there are one or two things we'd like to discuss and one or two explanations we need."

Before I could reply, his wife reached over and picked up the two cards.

"We'll do no such thing," she said. "Mr Thompson's come here for his lunch. We'll not have it spoilt by any silly talk."

What a good lunch it was.

Sir John Stokes MP

Member for Halesowen and Stourbridge

In 1935 at the Randolph Hotel, Oxford, at the age of eighteen, I attended my first important political dinner. I found myself sitting on the left of Sir Austen Chamberlain, the former Foreign Secretary and Knight of the Garter.

During our conversation he said, "I always feel sick before I make a speech."

This has often comforted me before making a speech.

Baroness Trumpington

Minister of State, Agriculture, Fisheries and Food

I went to a Conservative fund-raising party in a constituency where I knew nobody. In desperation I went up to a strange man and said, "I'm mingling."

"What a funny name," he said. "How do you do, Mrs Mingling.

Tony Baldry MP

*Member for Banbury, Parliamentary Under-Secretary of State,
Department of the Environment*

On Becoming a Minister

In January 1990, the Prime Minister asked me to go to the Department of Energy as a Junior Minister, where amongst other things I had responsibility for the electricity industry.

It was quite clear to our son's teacher that Edward, aged six, was somewhat distracted in the days immediately after my arrival at the Department of Energy. On making tactful enquiries as to why he appeared a little upset, Edward replied, "I am worried about Daddy and I am worried about the lights. Mummy said, 'I don't know what the Prime Minister is doing giving Daddy any responsibility for the electricity industry. He can't even change a plug!' "

Mother of Parliaments

Ken Hargreaves MP
Member for Hyndburn

On the Terrace of the House of Commons, when pointing out St Thomas' Hospital on the other side of the river, I am usually reminded of an incident which occurred soon after my becoming a Member of Parliament.

I was standing in the Central Lobby one evening with Jeremy Hanley. We were approached by two nurses from St Thomas' Hospital who explained that they were on a treasure hunt and would get five bonus points if they collected two MPs. Filled with a feeling of importance and a desire to help, we returned to the hospital with them only to find that they would have been given eight bonus points if they collected a Mars Bar wrapper.

So much for the importance of MPs!

David Evans MP
Member for Welwyn Hatfield

Shortly after my election, I ran into a certain young Minister, whom I had known for many years. He looked ten years older than when I had last seen him six months before. His eyes were staring, his hair was standing on end and he was carrying sufficient files and papers to have been able to save the entire Rain Forests himself.

"Slow down," I said. "Rome wasn't built in a day."

"Maybe not," he replied, "but it would have been if Margaret Thatcher had been in charge."

The Rt Hon the Lord Boyd-Carpenter
(MP *for Kingston upon Thames 1945-72, Chief Secretary to The Treasury 1962-64*)

When Sir Winston Churchill was leading the Opposition in the 1945 Parliament, he delivered a speech fiercely critical of the Labour Party which made a Labour Member, Mr Paling, shout at him, "Dirty dog!"

Without hesitation, Churchill swung round and said, "The Honourable Member knows what dirty dogs do to palings."

Sir Anthony Kershaw
(MP *for Stroud 1955-87*)

Corporal Major Jackson, ex-Life Guards, doorkeeper at the House of Commons, on the occasion when Miss Mintoff threw horse manure from the gallery on to the floor of the House, said:

"Colonel, that horse needs a good bran mash."

69

A few months later a woman threw red paint on to the floor. Corporal Major Jackson looked at it and said to me:

"Colonel, I prefer horse shit."

The Rt Hon the Lord Boardman

(MP *for Leicester South West* 1967-74, *Chief Secretary to the Treasury* 1974)

Having won my Seat at a by-election, I was waiting for a favourable opportunity to make my maiden speech. Before doing so, however, I thought I would try myself out with an Oral Question.

I selected a Question that had been tabled for the Prime Minister, Harold Wilson, on the Territorial Army, and hoped to be called with my Supplementary which I had carefully rehearsed and memorised. While the Question on the Order Paper was being answered, I saw that the Speaker was looking at me and felt sure I would be called next.

As the Prime Minister sat down, the Speaker, looking straight at me, called, "Mr Silvester". Fred Silvester had won a by-election just before me. He remained in his seat looking very worried. There was a pause. The Speaker then realised his error and called, "Mr Tom Boardman". As I stood up, my mind went completely blank but, fortunately, by the time I was upright my memory had returned just in time for me to ask my Supplementary.

That brief period of blankness as I rose to my feet seemed like an age, and I shall never forget it.

Sir Kenneth Lewis

(*MP for Rutland and Stamford* 1959-83, *Stamford and Spalding* 1983-87)

Early in January 1983 just after I had received a Knighthood in the New Year's Honours List, I happened to have a question down to the Prime Minister, Mrs Margaret Thatcher.

When I stood up to put the question, and before I could actually put it, the Member for Christchurch, Mr Robert Adley interrupted to say, "Never mind (the question) Kenneth, just say 'thank you!' "

After that, nothing I said, whatever question it was, mattered at all. The Chamber was dissolved in laughter.

It is time my friend Robert Adley was knighted!

John Greenway MP
Member for Ryedale

It is not always appreciated that Ryedale includes part of the Rowntree Mackintosh York chocolate factory and the historic Rowntree Quaker village of New Earswick. The Nestlé takeover bid for Rowntree in 1988 was one of my first major political tests.

I managed to secure an adjournment debate to press the then Trade and Industry Secretary, Lord Young, to refer the matter to the Monopolies and Mergers Commission, only to find that Lord Young announced his intention not to do so on the morning of the debate. Nevertheless, with local interest at fever pitch, BBC Radio York agreed to take a direct line from the BBC Parliamentary Unit from midnight when the day's business – the report stage of the Firearms Bill – was due to end. When the guillotine fell, over forty amendments had not even been discussed.

Opponents to the Bill then forced a division on every single amendment. This is such a time-consuming process that the Deputy Speaker, Sir Paul Dean, was then persuaded to allow a rarely-used procedure of MPs standing in their places to register their votes rather than trip through the lobbies.

My long-awaited adjournment thus began at 5.30 am, by which time, of course, Radio York listeners had long since gone to bed! However it did make a good headline in the local evening paper: "Dawn Fury in Commons over Rowntree."

The following evening, at a constituency function, the Rowntree takeover not surprisingly was the main topic of conversation. In the usual custom, my wife drew the raffle and pulled out one of *my* tickets. The prize? A box of Rowntree Mackintosh Black Magic!

Someone kindly took a photograph of Sylvia presenting me with the box of chocolates and I keep this photograph in my wallet as a reminder of the week's events.

The Rt Hon the Lord Renton

(MP *for Huntingdon* 1945-79, *Minister of State, Home Office* 1961-62)

A Couple of Parliamentary Incidents

James Stuart of Findhorn, Secretary of State for Scotland, when asked in the Commons to speak up, said, "I'm most awfully sorry. I didn't know anyone was listening!"

Then there was Harry Cruickshank, Leader of the Commons in 1951 in Winston Churchill's last administration. When asked if the Government had found any skeletons in the cupboard on taking over from their predecessors, he replied, "Oh no! They were hanging from the chandeliers."

Patrick Cormack MP

Member for Staffordshire South

About ten years ago a deputation came to see me from my local District Council on a matter of high and serious importance. I waited for them on the steps at St Stephen's entrance and was somewhat perplexed when one of the sober-suited, briefcase-carrying brigade expressed

73

some apprehension at going through security. I had to persuade him, firmly but gently, that an elected Councillor, however exalted, could not go through without having his briefcase checked. He seemed ready to opt out of the deputation altogether when he was almost carried forward by two of his colleagues who had rather knowing grins on their faces.

"He's been shopping, I think," one of them whispered to me as they went by.

We soon all discovered that he had indeed been shopping – and where. Inside his briefcase, which his colleagues craned forward to see, were a number of luridly packaged "adult aids" and catalogues.

There really should have been a medal for the attendant who, without showing a flicker of amusement, or any other emotion, quickly closed the case and said, "Just your papers, and toys for the children I see, sir."

Sydney Chapman MP

Member for Chipping Barnet, Lord Commissioner

I was speaking in the House of Commons on the 20th January on a British Railways Bill which involved demolition of a viaduct which would restore the historic prospect from Ludgate Circus of Wren's masterpiece, St Paul's Cathedral:

"I can say that Christopher Wren and myself have two things in common – we were both architects and MPs. It was realised there might be a personality clash, so it was eventually agreed between our agents that Sir Christopher would promise to make no more political speeches if I promised to design no more buildings. I must say, Mr

Speaker, the arrangement seems to have stood the test of time."

Sir Robert Rhodes James MP
Member for Cambridge

A maiden speech in the House of Commons is a terrifying ordeal – at least, I found it so. I was so nervous that I typed it all out, so that if my nerves became too much I could read it out. The trouble was it was too long, a point most vividly and characteristically put to me by Ted Heath after I had sat down, when he remarked, "Congratulations on *both* your maiden speeches!"

Since then I have always spoken briefly, and never for more than ten minutes. I have always been grateful to Ted for his kind hint – and so, I strongly suspect, has the House of Commons.

Sir Kenneth Lewis
(MP *for Rutland and Stamford* 1959-83, *Stamford and Spalding* 1983-87)

When I first became an MP in 1959 as a new Member, my visits to the Members' Dining Room in the evening provided an opportunity to look at Cabinet Ministers sitting at their special Cabinet Table. It was a long tradition that Ministers, even some who were not in the Cabinet, supped together. Other Members sat at tables round the side of the room. But before I arrived at

Westminster, some Ministers had begun to leave the Cabinet Table and join other MPs round the room.

I knew many of these Ministers because we had all been candidates in the late 1940s and early 1950s. One of them was the redoubtable Tyneside Member, Dame Irene Ward, to whom I expressed the opinion that the Cabinet Table was now outdated – not in keeping with the Harold Macmillan large-majority, all-comrades-together administration.

If I, a new member, had the nerve to sit at the Cabinet Table, would she join me, I asked Dame Irene. Always one for a political lark she said, "What a splendid idea." We fixed a Wednesday evening the following week because Wednesdays are always good dining-in-the-House nights.

Dame Irene, in a splendid large hat, and I came into the Dining Room and walked smartly over to the Cabinet Table. I remember now only that I sat down next to Duncan

Sandys and Dr Charles Hill. They smiled broadly, passed us menus, and other Ministers clapped their hands in mock applause. MPs round the room, clearly, were pleasantly astonished.

I think the year was 1963. After that, the Cabinet Table became anyone's table and any table in the Dining Room available to Ministers, and at the end of that Parliamentary session, the Cabinet Table ceased to exist.

Andrew Mitchell MP
Member for Gedling

One of my favourite stories was told to me by Sir John Stradling Thomas MP on my first night as a Member of Parliament. Sir John was the former Member for Monmouth who is sadly no longer with us.

A young and rather precocious MP found himself in the Smoking Room of the House of Commons sitting next to Sir Winston Churchill after he had ceased to be Prime Minister and was in his twilight years as a Member of Parliament.

There had just been an unexpected vote in the House of Commons and the new MP had had to rush over from his office which was some distance from the House; he had only just made it into the Division Lobby in time.

"I ask you," said the young MP to Sir Winston, "there I was, rushing to vote, clearly in a hurry, and the policeman wouldn't stop the traffic until I told him who I was."

"Oh really," said Sir Winston, "and who were you?"

The Viscount Davidson

Captain of the Queen's Bodyguard of the Yeoman of the Guard

As we have no Speaker in the House of Lords, it is the duty of the Government Whip on the Front Bench to keep order. (This is necessary only on very rare occasions!)

One such occurred when I was Home Office Whip some years ago. During a late hour debate, one of the Bishops got up to speak and moved into the aisle. The Clerk at the Table pointed out to me that this was out of order. As it was unlikely that anyone would wish to walk up or down the aisle at such a late hour, I decided to take no action.

After the House was up, I ran into the Bishop in the Princes Chamber and mentioned (with due deference) that he had been out of order.

"My dear boy," he said, "I know I was, but there was a terrible draught coming up my surplice."

Sir Reg Prentice

(MP for Daventry 1979-87, Minister for Social Security 1979-81)

P arliament was in recess when I crossed the floor in October 1977. My press statement said that I had resigned from the Labour Party, applied to join the Conservatives and would 'apply for the Conservative whip' at the start of the new session.

Reporting this, Radio Piccadilly in Manchester were a little mixed up. They announced, "Mr Prentice has joined the Conservative Party and applied for the job of Chief Whip."

When I told Humphrey Atkins, Chief Whip at the time, he exclaimed, "What a marvellous idea!" – but fortunately he decided to carry on.

Sir Robert Rhodes James MP

Member for Cambridge

W hen Papua New Guinea became independent in 1978, the then Prime Minister, Jim Callaghan, solemnly moved that a Commons delegation be sent to attend this auspicious occasion, taking with it a clock to be presented to the Papua New Guinea Parliament.

The House was hushed and reverent, and Margaret Thatcher and Jeremy Thorpe spoke in the same grave tones about our links with Papua New Guinea, our pride in its peoples' independence, the importance of parliamentary democracy, and all that. The House was at its most portentous. Then, from a far back bench Nicky Fairbairn rose. "As the clock concerned was made in Germany . . ." he began. There was a moment of consternation, and then gales of laughter, the whole funereal and grave atmosphere immediately and blessedly, punctured.

The Front Benches were not at all amused – and even less so when it was discovered that the clock was, in fact, British. But no one else cared very much, and Nicky was the back-benchers' hero of the hour.

Sir Kenneth Lewis

(MP for Rutland and Stamford 1959-83, Stamford and Spalding 1983-87)

When Sir Alec Douglas Home became Prime Minister in 1963, he brought Selwyn Lloyd back as Leader of the House.

There had been, for some time, much concern that there was no room in the House of Commons for Members' families to sit while waiting for their husbands or fathers. They had to wait in the Central Lobby. Selwyn said to me that the Services Committee would have to make some room available but there didn't seem to be a suitable room.

"What about the Geordie Room?" I said.

"Never heard of it!" he replied.

I said, "It's perfect for a Families Room – just off the Inner Lobby, adjacent to the Central Lobby."

Selwyn said, "I know the Medical Red Cross Room. There can't be another. Never seen it."

I showed him the room, with all the papers laid out and the comfortable leather chairs, a good place to sleep in on a late night. Selwyn couldn't believe his eyes. "How can I get the Geordies out – you'll have to help – this is obviously a matter for Diplomacy and not Gun Boat Action."

"A question of providing the Geordie Trade Union members with a suitable alternative," I replied. The Geordie/Trade Union Room is now opposite the Smoking Room and more than half the MPs still don't know it is there. Not surprising – there are now well over one thousand rooms in the Palace of Westminster.

The House of Commons got it's Families Room, a splendid contribution by Selwyn Lloyd to the comfort of MPs' families: the room he didn't even know existed.

Ken Hargreaves MP
Member for Hyndburn

While taking groups of constituents through the Division Lobby, I usually tell the visitors about two letters which I received from schoolchildren after a visit to the House of Commons.

The first, from a small boy said: "Dear Mr Hargreaves, Thank you for wasting your time showing us round the House of Commons."

The second, from a little girl, said that she had enjoyed her visit very much, but "couldn't understand how the eyes voted in a different Lobby to the nose."

The Rt Hon the Baroness Oppenheim-Barnes

(MP for Gloucester 1970-87, Minister of State for Consumer Affairs 1979-82)

I think my worst and certainly my most embarrassing gaffe as a very new Member occurred late one night before I had found my dearly beloved 'pair' of the past six and a half years, Tom Torney. I was standing at the entrance to the Chamber, the hour was very late and I was very tired. I glanced at the Member standing next to me who seemed to be similarly afflicted and thoroughly fed up. I judged him to be a member of the Labour Party. I plucked up courage and spoke up.

"Wouldn't you like to go home to bed?" I enquired pleadingly. He looked quite startled and not a little apprehensive. "Couldn't we pair?" I went on.

"My dear Sally," he replied. "Yes, I would like to go home to bed with you – no, we can't pair because we're both on the same side."

Was my face red!

Only a few days later, it was to become even redder, through no fault of mine this time. Again, late at night, just as I was getting into my car to wend my weary way home at the end of a very long day, I was hailed by Greville Janner.

"You have to pass my house on your way home," he said. "Could you drop me off, there don't seem to be any taxis."

Knowing Greville to be a perfect gentlemen (I thought) and knowing members of his family for years, I readily agreed. Imagine my embarrassment the next day to hear Greville's voice ring out across the tea-room, clearly heard by all:

"I left my hat in your car last night, Sally." Great merriment all round. My impeccable reputation was all but ruined. Little did I know that there was worse in store.

During an all night sitting, three colleagues and I had been playing bridge (in a private room). So engrossing was the game that we all failed to notice that the House was adjourned. The result was that some time later and with some difficulty we managed to contact a night security guard who let us out as dawn was breaking. By that time there really were no taxis and it was pelting with rain.

The then Prime Minister's PPS – one of the bridge players – recalled that he was expected to attend a very early meeting at Downing Street and would not have time to go home first. Consequently, he asked me to drop him at Number 10 on my way. This time I thought there could be no embarrassing repercussions – there would be no-one around so early in the morning. I drove into Downing Street in the pouring rain, dropped him off and beat a hasty retreat home.

Imagine my dismay to read in one of the gossip columns a day later, "Mystery blonde leaves Downing Street in early hours of the morning!"

That was positively the last time I ever gave *anyone* a lift!

Canvassing Blues

The Rt Hon Sir Bernard Braine MP
Member for Castle Point

Out of the mouths of babes . . .
When I was canvassing in my constituency some years ago, a very small boy answered my knock at the door.

"Is your Mummy in?" I enquired.

"No, sir, she's out."

"Is your Daddy in?"

"No, he's out as well."

I asked him to give his parents a leaflet carrying a personal message from me.

"Oh yes," he said brightly. "Mummy and Daddy vote for you."

As I said goodbye and started to turn away, I noticed a poster pinned to the wall depicting my Labour opponent. I pointed to it and said, "I thought you told me that your Mummy and Daddy voted for me?"

Looking over his shoulder distastefully at the poster, the little chap screwed his face up and said, "Oh that – my Mummy says, 'I'll grow up to look like him if I don't eat my dinner!' "

84

Simon Coombs MP

Member for Swindon

M ost canvassers must have been caught out at one time or another by the tendency of the Electoral Register to split the occupants of a house into two separate columns, so that the residents end up on successive canvass cards.

In the 1966 General Election, I was the second canvasser to call on a house in Reading on behalf of Peter Emery, who was defending a majority of ten. In reply to my initial question came the answer, "Oh no, we've been done already tonight."

Having established the problem, I ended my lengthy apologies with what I thought was an elegant phrase, "I'm afraid there has been some duplication of labour."

"Oh no," was the reply.

"Definitely, Conservative."

Baroness Blatch

Parliamentary Under-Secretary of State, Department of the Environment

D uring the time I was leader of Cambridgeshire County Council, I was canvassing for a friend who was standing as a Conservative in a local District Council Election, when a man in his forties came to the door.

After explaining why I was there and giving good reasons why he should vote Conservative, he exclaimed, "What – with the state of education and that bloody woman Emily Blatch."

"I am that bloody woman Emily Blatch," I replied.

"You're not are you?"

"Yes I am," I said, "and what particularly worries you?"

I finally withdrew leaving him lost for words and just a touch embarrassed.

The Conservatives won the district seat handsomely.

Dudley Fishburn MP

Member for Kensington

Knocking on doors of some of the grander houses in Kensington during my by-election, I found myself confronted by a butler in white gloves and tails.

"And how will this house be voting?" I asked.

"Well, sir," said the butler, drawing himself to his full height, "Madam wants it to be known that she is somewhat disillusioned with the Conservatives."

"And you?"

"Ah well, guv, I'm with you all the way. Couldn't afford to be otherwise."

Sir Richard Body MP

Member for Holland with Boston

"**Y**ou Tories can get stuffed," shouted a cantankerous old girl across a crowded street to my fellow canvasser who I knew was several months pregnant.

"Look," she retorted as she raised up her shirt, "I am stuffed."

Of the several who overheard the encounter, I am told two or three changed their vote to Tory. If that is a comment on the fickleness of the electorate, it is also a reminder that humour beats abuse.

Edwina Currie MP

Member for Derbyshire South
(Under-Secretary of State for Health 1986-88)

One of my favourite stories concerns Lady Astor, first woman to take her seat in the House of Commons and doyenne of women Tory MPs.

She and Admiral Beatty were out canvassing in Plymouth in the 1922 Election. As it was getting dark and they were in rather a rough area, they decided to pack up, but just to do a few more houses.

She knocked: a surly woman came to the door.

"Evening ma'am, sir," she said before either could utter a word. "Up the stairs and first on the right. That will be two guineas."

"I'm Lady Astor, your MP," protested the startled Nancy.

"I don't care about that," said the woman, "My husband says, when the lady comes with the sailor to show them upstairs and make sure they pay!"

Roger King MP

Member for Birmingham Northfield

During a General Election campaign, I was followed around on the time-honoured task of door-to-door canvassing by a West German television crew. Armed with a camera, sound boom, a floodlight and the necessary hangers on, this small army sought to record for posterity the uniqueness of my approach.

I espied two elderly ladies conversing on a doorstep. Quick as a flash, I bounded up to them. "Hello, I'm Roger King," etc. etc. A few moments later with a crashing and a clanking the film crew arrived, thrusting a sound boom in the general direction of the ladies while the floodlight added further brilliance to a beautiful June morning.

"What's all this then?" queried one of the ladies.

"Oh, don't mind them, they're a West German film crew from Hamburg finding out how we electioneer," I replied.

The camera whirred on.

"Ooah, fancy," came the response. "My Albert flew there once, dropped his load and came back."

Michael Jack MP

Member for Fylde, Parliamentary Under-Secretary of State, Department of Social Security

My wife had this experience when canvassing. She made the traditional approach of asking the voter whether he would be supporting me in the General Election campaign, to which he replied, "I've had enough of those damn Tories – I'm voting Conservative next time."

Sir Robert McCrindle MP

Member for Brentwood and Ongar

I was canvassing in an area of east London, close to the then thriving docks. I rang the bell which turned out to be one of those musical devices which play the favourite tune of the resident. To my horror the unmistakable tones of *The Red Flag* assailed my ears. It was too late to run.

So when a burly docker appeared on the doorstep, I timorously enquired his voting intentions. Clearly, offended by my implication that he might vote for anyone but the Tory candidate, he said, "I'm with you mate," and shut the door.

I've often wondered what reception I would get from a house where the doorbell played *Land of Hope and Glory*.

The Rt Hon Cranley Onslow MP

*Member for Woking, Chairman of the 1922 Committee
(Minister, Foreign Office 1982-3)*

Some years ago, when I was out canvassing in the Dartford area, I met an elderly man who said, "I want to show you this," and he pulled from his wallet an old card which he handed to me.

I saw it was headed *The Socialist Creed.*

"You'd better read it," said the chap, and so I did. This is what I read:

> *Comrades, let us get together and pool everything we own and share it out equally between us.*
> *And when I've spent my share, we'll do it again.*

Martin Graham

Deputy Director, Conservative Research Department

True Blues

Canvassing one particular block of flats was proving heavy-going. I rang another door bell and out came a rather elderly lady. She proceeded to inform me that she was none other than Queen Victoria's grand-daughter, except that people didn't seem to recognise blue blood when they saw it. I began to think of fruitcake. She was also, apparently, the victim of a massive fraud, whereby the City Council owed her two million pounds (that I could believe: Labour Council). And she had been swindled out of a vast estate. I pointed out re-assuringly that the

90

Conservative Party had a fine record on monarchy. This seemed to help. Yes, she would vote for us this time, "although strictly, royals shouldn't vote: they are supposed to be above politics." It took a certain amount of effort to ensure that my expression continued to reflect the gravity of the conversation. But I held out to the end and finally made my apologies.

The next one had to be an easier canvass. I rang the doorbell. As an elderly lady was opening the door, another neighbour poked her head into the corridor and volunteered, "you won't have a very easy time with her . . . she's deaf and dumb."

Sir Robert Rhodes James MP

Member for Cambridge

Canvassing produces oddities. One lady in Cambridge said she would never vote for me "because you were born in India".

When I pointed out that my father was an officer in the Indian Army and my mother was with him at the time and it was hardly my fault, she responded:

"I don't care. It's an 'orrible country to be born in."

Meanwhile, another lady was telling my wife with great vehemence that she would never vote Conservative "because of what you did over the Zinoviev Letter". Voters have long memories, and not always very helpful ones.

As I am the historian in the family, my wife asked me what on earth this vehement voter was talking about and I explained that she had been referring to the 1924 General Election.

The Rt Hon Sir Ian Stewart MP

Member for Hertfordshire North
(Minister of State for Northern Ireland 1988-1989)

When I was canvassing in my first election in Hitchin in 1974, I discovered that democracy was a more complicated business than I had realised.

One constituent, when asked if he would support me, replied very politely, "I vote for each of the three main parties in turn, but I am afraid I never say whose turn it is to be lucky."

Sir John Wheeler MP
Member for Westminster North

As is well known, the oldest profession practises its arts in my constituency. I was calling upon expensive rented property owned by the Church Commissioners. A very attractive young lady answered the door and invited me to step into the apartment, wherein I found a "client".

Naturally, I ignored the circumstances and politely enquired if I could expect the occupants to favour the Party with their votes. The girl assured me that she was resolute in her support for free enterprise. The client somewhat disappointingly, I thought, assured me of everything, as long as I left!

Sir Peter Emery MP
Member for Honiton

In canvassing at the Ribble Valley by-election, I was inundated with complaints, many from previous Conservative supporters, about the Community Charge or "that damned poll tax" as it was so often referred to on the doorstep. Therefore, after half an hour of little success, I was delighted when a man came to the door and said, "Ah, you're from the Conservatives ?"

I rapidly answered, "Yes."

"Oh, good," said he. "I've supported private enterprise all my life."

At that moment, two men, who appeared to be familiar with the owner of the house, came forward and stood on the front step and closed the front door. They each took hold of my Conservative supporter by the arms.

One of them turned to me and said, "I don't think he'll be out by Thursday, guvner," and proceeded swiftly to put him into a police car.

My only apparent success was seen disappearing down the road!

The Rt Hon the Lord Jenkin of Roding
(MP *for Wanstead and Woodford 1964-87, Secretary of State for the Environment 1983-1985*)

Tory canvasser (brightly) to small, mousy man who has answered the door:

"Well, my man, and which party do you belong to?"

Voice from the rear of the house: "I'm the party 'e belongs to!"

David Madel MP
Member for Bedfordshire South West

I was canvassing a certain road with one of my supporters. In a front garden, was a very large and very beautiful golden labrador. He looked at my supporter asking her to scratch him behind the ears, and she duly obliged. The dog had got to the stage of giving her a large wet lick, when the owner came to the front door.

We asked if his politics were the same as his dog's, to which he replied, "Yes, good dog that one. He growled at the Liberal and bit the Socialist!"

on the other hand . . . .

Jim Lester MP
Member for Broxtowe

During the 1983 election, I was canvassing with my President. As he was preparing to put our election literature through a front door, the dog of the household came out, took it from his hand and proceeded to tear it into shreds.

A short while after, the lady of the house came out and enquired whether we were Labour or Conservative. When we said Conservative, she patted the dog and said, "Good dog, good dog."

John Hannam MP

Member for Exeter

At the last General Election I knocked on a door and a little woman answered. As I was explaining who I was, a loud voice called out from inside the house, "Who is it?"

The woman called back to her husband, "It's the Conservative candidate."

A bellow came back, "Tell him to b . . . . . off," and a huge bare-armed man appeared, shaking his fists.

As I retreated gracefully down the garden path, I looked back. The little lady was standing just behind her threatening husband, giving me the "thumbs up" sign and a warm smile of encouragement.

That was certainly a household which the husband mistakenly considered safe for two Labour votes!

Sir Paul Hawkins

(MP for Norfolk North West 1963-83)

In January 1955, John Hill fought a difficult by-election in South Norfolk, not least for myself, trying to help.

After a day in sleet and snow visiting isolated farms and villages, we arrived in the dark at our last destination, where we were to be an 'Any Questions Panel'.

Missing the way, I turned at a 'one pump' garage. Grazing the pump, I watched with horror as the 'globe' crashed to the ground, which brought more of the village out than came to our meeting. Finally, we got the Village Hall – nothing but a Nissen hut with concrete floor and one oil stove.

Afterwards, we were invited to the Chairlady's home for coffee and refreshments. Her husband, obviously (and actually) a retired Colonel, had on retirement become a pig farmer and at that time pig prices were on the floor. He loudly announced, "Even if my stupid wife votes Conservative, I certainly shall not!"

Getting into a cold bed after midnight, I wondered how many votes we had lost besides the garage owner's. Thank Goodness, John won by a narrow margin!

The Rt Hon Sir Nicholas Lyell MP

Member for Bedfordshire Mid
(MP *for Hemel Hempstead* 1979-83)

Canvassing the Unexpected

Canvassing during the 1983 General Election campaign, I introduced myself to a woman quietly gardening in front of her house.

"How do you do," I said. "I am your new Conservative candidate in the election."

"Not mine," she said in a tone of voice which boded ill for an extra vote.

"Who do you support?" I asked.

"The Communists, only there isn't one," she replied, looking round as though trying to keep an eye on someone or something.

"Do you have any children?" I said, hoping to seem friendly even to the opposition.

"No," she replied, "a snake!"

And there I saw it, entwined round the rose trellis, tongue flickering, almost within reach – a four foot python. I moved on!

Sir Peter Mills

(MP *for Torrington* 1964-74, *Devon West* 1974-83, *Torridge and West Devon* 1983-87, *Parliamentary Under-Secretary of State for Northern Ireland* 1972-1974)

An Identity Problem

Canvassing in a small Devon village, I was wearing my blue rosette, which had in the middle of it the name 'Peter Mills'. I was carrying a sheaf of Conservative blue literature. I knocked at one house and spoke to the lady who came to the door.

"I am Peter Mills, the Conservative candidate," I said, and went through the usual routine.

When I had finished, she paused and then replied: "Yes, Jeremy Thorpe, I never did like this man Peter Mills much, and I will vote for you!"

The Rt Hon Sir William Clark MP

Member for Croydon South

My wife and I were canvassing on opposite sides of a road. My wife called at a house and was invited in, but she demurred. The lady was insistent. She said she had been waiting to meet my wife and would like to show her her budgerigar, in the far corner of the room. My wife walked over to it. Nothing happened; it seemed perfectly happy. But after a few seconds the lady announced, "The budgerigar likes you, I shall vote for your husband."

I have to admit that I was not successful at that election. There evidently weren't enough budgies in the constituency!

Kenneth Warren MP

Member for Hastings and Rye

Canvassing a street furiously at a General Election in Hastings, my team was going ahead getting people to their doorsteps for me to rush up and greet them.

I ran up one garden path to a frail lady in a dressing-gown and shook her warmly by the hand. I pulled my hand away with a gasp thinking I had been bitten by a dog. I looked down and saw that in her hand she was holding her dentures.

Elections – The Acid Test

Rupert Allason MP
Member for Torbay

During the 1979 General Election my father very kindly offered to bring some of his friends to help campaign in the Kettering constituency where I was the candidate. One evening, while canvassing on an estate in what was then a particularly rough part of Corby, which was itself a very tough steel town, I overheard the following monologue:

"Good evening sir, I'm sorry to trouble you while you're dressing for dinner, but I'm the former Greek Ambassador to London, and I'm calling on behalf of Rupert Allason who is standing at the Election.

"Of course, I don't have a vote in this country . . . but if I did I would probably give it to him. I can't say I know him frightfully well, but his father plays a very decent game of bridge at White's Club most evenings, and if he's anything like his father, Rupert would probably be worth supporting . . ."

I quickly intervened and found a less demanding role for my father's friends in the remainder of the campaign which I lost by a narrow margin.

Sydney Chapman MP

Member for Chipping Barnet, Lord Commissioner

I was MP for Handsworth from 1970 to 1974, when demographic and boundary changes ensured my defeat.

Turning to the Returning Officer (Lord Mayor of Birmingham) after my defeat was announced, I said, "Finally, My Lord Mayor, let me say that the only distinction I had in the last Parliament was to be the only architect in the House of Commons. Tonight, therefore, I reckon I'm the only failed politician who can say with literal truth: "Ah well, back to the drawing-board.""

Alastair Goodlad MP

Member for Eddisbury, Deputy Chief Whip

During the 1970 General Election, as the Conservative Parliamentary candidate in Crewe, I arrived to speak at one of my widely advertised public meetings to find only 9oe person in the audience, an elderly lady.

A snap decision had to be taken as to whether to deliver my carefully prepared oration or have a friendly chat. I decided that since the lady had made the effort to come to the meeting she should be given her money's worth. Having doubled the size of the audience by asking my wife to sit in the body of the hall, I spoke for some twenty minutes on the deficiencies of the then Labour Government and the promise of better things to come in the event of a Conservative victory. I then invited questions.

The only one forthcoming was, "When does the Women's Institute meeting begin?"

The Rt Hon Edward Heath MP

Member for Old Bexley and Sidcup
(Prime Minister 1970-74)

It is a tradition in Bexley that the last meeting of a General Election campaign should be held at a hall in the old village which, under its deeds, can only be used by a Conservative candidate.

After a strenuous and exhausting campaign, I arrived to find the hall packed and a large crowd of people trying to cram themselves through the doors.

All our meetings had been organised very efficiently by the Young Conservatives, who were also responsible for this final rally. All the YC helpers had gathered there from all the wards and were thickly lining the back of the wall, ready to deal with any difficulties. In fact, the audience was in good humour and required no disciplinary action from the YCs who promptly turned their attention to my speech which they had now heard some eighteen times. For this new development I was quite unprepared.

After a brief introduction I rapidly moved to the individual issues facing us at the Election, and particularly in Bexley. Foremost amongst them was housing. I compared the situation when the Borough was built with the appalling lack of new housing under the post-war Labour Government.

"Let me remind you," I started, "that most of the Borough of Bexley was built . . ."

"Between 1926 and 1936," came a roar from the back, completely drowning my own words.

"And when you look at the end of a row of houses you can still see the price painted up on the wall."

"£375," came a roar from the back.

By now I thought it was better to make this a duologue.

"And so what deposit was necessary?" I enquired.

"Just £5," responded the roar of the YCs.

I was left in no doubt that those who had listened to my speech had certainly taken it all on board.

Vivian Bendall MP

Member for Ilford North

Towards the end of Polling Day in the 1983 General Election, we knocked on the door of a house where two pledges had not yet voted. The lady of the house was quite agitated about getting to the polling station on time.

She called to her husband, telling him to drop everything as they must go straight away. She came out of the house very quickly, pulling on a jacket, and promptly fell heavily, landing on her arm. She had in fact broken her arm but insisted that she would vote before going on to the hospital.

After the election was over, I visited her and signed her plaster cast.

Sir Patrick McNair-Wilson MP

Member for New Forest

At my Adoption Meeting as Prospective Parliamentary Candidate for the New Forest in 1968, the Association President was explaining why I had been selected from a short list which included The Rt Hon Sir Geoffrey Howe QC, MP and Sir Anthony Meyer Bt, MC, MP.

He pointed out to the audience of some three hundred, that with Britain's largest oil refinery in the constituency, at Fawley, it was necessary to have a candidate with some knowledge of the industry. I had been an Opposition Front Bench Spokesman on Energy until the General Election in 1966, when I lost my seat at West Lewisham.

He ended his persuasive remarks with a flourish, declaring, ". . . and ladies, and gentlemen, I can assure you that no one knows more about the oil industry than your new candidate – Patrick Gordon Walker."

Stunned silence, followed by great amusement.

Patrick Gordon Walker had been appointed as Foreign Secretary by Harold Wilson, in advance of his fighting a by-election which he had recently lost.

Baroness Blatch

Parliamentary Under-Secretary of State, Department of the Environment

During the referendum on Britain's entry into Europe, I was visiting a residential home for the elderly. While chatting with the staff in the day room, I was asked if, as I walked around, I would collect up the postal votes to be returned to the local council office. It was mid-morning and coincided with coffee and biscuit time. When I asked one elderly lady if she had completed her form she replied, "Yes," but it was nowhere to be seen.

Her friend sitting close by said, "She's eaten it!"

On a closer look, it was obvious that what I thought were biscuit crumbs on her lap were in fact soggy pieces of beige-coloured card. She had indeed eaten it!

Sir Robert Rhodes James MP

Member for Cambridge

One of the features of Cambridge elections is, or used to be, open air soapbox meetings in the Market Place, and which I undertook on Saturday mornings for several years, usually to a huge and not too supportive a crowd. Once, I was supported by Francis Pym and John Peyton. I was in full cry when a drunk came lurching towards me, waving a bottle, and saying deeply unpleasant things. John touched me on the arm, and said, "Don't worry, it's half full!" Here was the authentic voice of the experienced professional politician.

At the declaration of my by-election victory in 1976, on the balcony outside the Cambridge Guildhall, some enraged Socialists did throw empty bottles. They fairly rained on us and crashed against the wall, as our Agent hurriedly got us off. My Labour chums were very contrite, explaining that they weren't aiming at us, but at the National Front candidate, and, "as we haven't much experience of this sort of thing" their aim was bad. I retorted, forgivingly, that this was no consolation at all, and I would be grateful if this custom could cease. It did.

My charming Liberal opponent in 1979 took a leaf out of my book by doing a soapbox meeting in the Market Place. When he asked for questions, a fourteen-year-old girl asked, "If the Liberals are so great, how is it that they haven't been in office for fifty years?"

The crowd roared, "Answer!" and my Liberal friend was flummoxed by the little pest.

She was our youngest daughter. We hurriedly pulled her out of the campaign before her identity was rumbled, but her intervention is still fondly remembered in Cambridge, even by the victim. She is now a fine young actress, who was once turned down for a part as the daughter of a Tory MP because she "did not look like the daughter of a Tory MP", which she, and we, thought was a bit rough. What did they expect daughters of Tory MPs to look like? Therein lies a mystery.

The Rt Hon Julian Amery MP

Member for Brighton Pavilion
(Minister for Foreign and Commonwealth Affairs 1972-74)

I spent my honeymoon in Preston fighting the General Election of 1950.

We saw from the start that it would be a close run thing. But all the world loves a young couple; and

Catherine's presence on my platform swung many votes to me. At one meeting, in our worst ward, an old-fashioned type of working man, unshaven and wearing a scarf and cloth cap, asked me what time I got up in the morning. I answered that I rose at eight.

He shouted back, "Eight! You lazy bastard. Why I get up at five every morning."

Another man of much the same type got up two rows behind. He turned to his mate and, pointing to Catherine, said to him, "Yer wouldn't if yer went to bed with yon."

The hall collapsed with laughter and we must have turned a dozen votes that night.

The Rt Hon the Viscount Whitelaw

(MP *for Penrith and Borders* 1955-83, *Deputy Leader of the Conservative Party* 1975-1991)

My Most Absurd Village Meeting

In a country district in Cumbria in the 1955 election, I went to the village hall at the necessary time, as instructed, accompanied by someone who was acting for me as Chairman. There were eight men sitting in the hall, all with their caps on, and totally motionless. We went to the table, the Chairman introduced me and I spoke.

The eight men's faces never moved at all, never appeared to take any notice of what was going on. They continued quietly, some smoking their pipes and some just sitting. At the end of the speech, the Chairman asked for questions – nobody moved a muscle. The Chairman thanked me for coming – nobody moved a muscle, and we left the room.

I have never known to this day whether I was attending an election meeting or whether I was attending some other occasion. However, I made certain that I would never have a meeting at that village at any subsequent election again, and didn't!

Ian Taylor MP

Member for Esher

Campaigning in the 1991 May elections, I came across one difficult constituent, who seemed to calm down while I explained the merits of the Conservative cause and of the Council candidate. He promised to vote Conservative.

The following week, the candidate again met the constituent who congratulated him on getting the Prime Minister himself to canvass for him! He could not be persuaded that he had only been talking to the Member of Parliament.

"It must have been the Prime Minister," he said conclusively, "because he was very nice . . ."

Jerry Hayes MP
Member for Harlow

After a heavy day's canvassing in the Portsmouth by-election in the early 80s, I decided to canvass one more block of flats. All went well until the very last door. This was opened by one of the tallest ladies that I have ever seen. Unperturbed, I embarked on the smooth politician's patter which became less smooth and more erratic the closer I looked at the lady. There was something not quite right; she was wearing a wig which was slightly askew, she was heavily made up, had a rather deep voice and an adam's apple the size of a ping-pong ball, and, oh dear, there were traces of a five o'clock shadow. I suddenly realised that this was a man dressed as a woman.

The smooth patter ground to a halt. "Er," I stammered, "Regarding your vote, what exactly are you?"

"Oh," came the response, "I've never really discovered quite what I am!"

The truest words spoken at that by-election.

Winston S Churchill MP

Member for Daveyhulme

D uring the 1964 General Election campaign I assisted
Ted Heath in his Bexley constituency. It was my first
active involvement in an election and I soon discovered the
hazards of political campaigning.

One morning, with a large team of party workers and a
couple of journalists from the national press, we were
canvassing a road of semi-detached houses. I had gone up
the path to ring a doorbell. The door was opened by a very
attractive young lady in a black diaphanous nightdress who,
seeing Ted coming up the path hard on my heels, greeted us
warmly with the words: "Good morning, gents! Won't you
please come in?"

I looked over my shoulder to see the candidate fleeing
down the path as fast as his legs could carry him.

The Rt Hon Sir Frederic Bennett

(MP *for Reading North 1951-55: Torquay 1955-74: Torbay 1974-
87)*

I shall always recall one incident during a General Election
campaign in Torbay. During a visit to a local residential
home, I had promised that I would personally take a ninety-
nine-year-old gentleman, whom I had known quite well
over the years, to the polling station.

Hence, on the morning of election day, together with my
secretary's sister, Christine, I called and helped the would-
be supporter slowly out to my car. And then came the
problem. How did we get the old chap, who was quite tall,
to bend his frame into the car?

We had been pondering this difficult situation for some time when the matron of the home came to our rescue, saying, "It is quite simple to get Mr X seated in the car." She proceeded to demonstrate this by giving him a sharp karate chop with one hand behind the knees, while using the other to force his body down into the seat as his knees buckled, and then swinging his legs quickly round into the car.

Safely in the car, we arrived at the Polling Station, where to our relief the task of getting him out was much simpler. But after he had voted, Christine and I looked wildly at one another, not sure who was going to do the 'necessary' to get him back into the car for the return journey. We decided on a joint effort, so while I administered the karate chop behind the knees, she forced him down into the car and swung his legs in as he buckled. I would be the first to admit that our effort was not as cleanly accomplished as that of the matron, and we both straightened up to find the horrified gaze of an audience of would-be voters making their way to the polling station. One could almost read their thoughts along the lines, "The Tory candidate seems rather desperate for votes."

I continue to wonder, having gained one vote, how many I lost in those few fateful seconds?

The Rt Hon the Lord Boyd-Carpenter

(MP *for Kingston upon Thames 1945-72, Chief Secretary to the Treasury 1962-64*)

At the 1945 General Election, to which I returned rather belatedly from service in Italy, our very efficient Town Clerk in Kingston got our result out second in the country.

Everyone at that time expected a general Conservative victory and there was some disappointment that my majority was not bigger than that of my predecessor at the by-election in 1937, at a bad time for the Party. They said consolingly, "One cannot expect better than this from a raw young candidate straight out of the Army."

By the evening, when the adjoining safe Conservative seats of Spelthorne and Wimbledon had gone Labour, those comments were, with some embarrassment, withdrawn and cherished bottles brought out and opened!

Sir Peter Mills MP

(MP for Torrington 1964-74, Devon West 1974-83, Torridge and West Devon 1983-87, Parliamentary Under-Secretary of State for Northern Ireland 1972-74)

The Worker and the Tree

During an election, one of my supporters was trying to put up a poster which said "*MILLS* – the Man for Torrington". Just as he was nailing the poster to a tree, he noticed a small round hole in the trunk and decided to have a look inside. There he saw four lovely little mouths opened wide, waiting to be fed.

Just at that moment, the mother owl came back and attacked him. Needless to say, he moved on to another tree!

Julian Brazier MP

Member for Canterbury

Leon Brittan had very kindly come up to support me as candidate in Berwick-on-Tweed in the 1983 General Election campaign. He was my first VIP visitor and we decided to start in a large picturesque village. To my absolute horror, as we progressed down the High Street, not one door was answered; after about twenty minutes, finally, a woman came to the door and, immediately recognising Leon Brittan, (who was Home Secretary) launched into a diatribe about the demonstration then taking place on the roof of the prison on the Isle of Wight.

She told us that she thought that hanging wasn't good enough for these prisoners, that they should feel a touch of the lash first, and then gave her imagination still fuller vent. Throughout this Leon maintained an equitable disposition, until a brief pause for breath on the woman's part provided him with an opportunity to ask, "Is there any other subject you would like to ask me about?"

Immediately the woman replied, "Yes, I am most concerned about cruelty to animals."

The Rt Hon Edward Heath MP

Member for Old Bexley and Sidcup
(*Prime Minister 1970-74*)

In my first General Election in Bexley, which was then in Kent, in February 1950, I spoke at three meetings a night. Towards the end of the campaign I arrived for the last meeting of the evening at a school to find the hall was packed with people, a large number of whom were engaged in rather a heated altercation with the chairman. I edged my way along the wall until I finally reached the Chairman's table, where I sat down on an empty chair, tugged his sleeve vigorously and said, "I am here, you know."

He looked at me somewhat surprised, but succeeded in calling the meeting to order, after which he said, "I now have to introduce the Conservative candidate." He picked up a sheet of paper with which he had been provided by the Agent and it was soon apparent from his halting delivery that he had certainly not taken the trouble to read it beforehand.

"The candidate was born in Kent," he started. This very relevant piece of information was heard in silence.

"The candidate went to school in Kent," he continued. This, too, was greeted by silence.

"The candidate has so far spent all his life in Kent," added the Chairman. At which a heckler at the back of the hall broke the silence by a shout:

"And for all I care, he can bloody well die in Kent!"

Harry Greenway MP

Member for Ealing North

Margaret Thatcher came to speak in my marginal constituency of Ealing North in the General Election campaign of 1983. The meeting took the form of a rally outside the Greenford Conservative Club and a large crowd was present. I had warmed up the crowd and there was great excitement as the election bus with Mrs Thatcher aboard was awaited. Several celebrity friends of mine were present in support of my campaign, among them John Conteh the world boxing champion, actors and actresses and Lord Taylor of Hadfield, founder of Taylor Woodrow.

An excited councillor, who has since passed to higher things, asked to be allowed to introduce the boxer and built him up with an impressive background of victories, to which would be added, he said, the 1983 General Election for the Conservative Party. He then announced, "I give you Mr Joe Bugner!"

An embarrassed John Conteh was left with the task of politely correcting the councillor.

The Rt Hon the Viscount Whitelaw

(MP *for Penrith and Borders* 1955-83, *Deputy Leader of the Conservative Party* 1975-1991)

A distinguished Conservative figure arrived to speak for me – a very innocent young candidate in my first election. There was an audience of some eight hundred in those days, quite normal on Clydeside, even at Conservative meetings. As soon as he started to speak, a typical character in a cloth cap and muffler shouted out, "Liar!"

The distinguished figure replied, "You will not call me that again."

A few minutes later, the man in the cloth cap shouted out again, "Liar!"

The distinguished figure: "You will not call me that again, and if you do I shall stop speaking and leave the hall. It is insulting for me to be treated like that."

Ten minutes passed, again the man in the cloth called out, "Liar!"

The distinguished figure got up, turned to me and said, "Your proposed constituents are not worthy of my attention, and I shall leave the meeting."

He did, leaving me to carry on – a very harsh introduction to electioneering.

Greg Knight MP
Member for Derby North, Lord Commissioner

Some of our politicians have their first taste of political battle whilst still at school, and I was no exception. During the 1966 General Election, I stood as the Conservative candidate at a mock election being held at my school. Initially, attempts were made to make the election as realistic as possible and each of the candidates was expected, in turn, to address the whole school, on the subject of their manifesto.

Previous campaigns at the school had been fairly professional affairs, having been organised by a science teacher, who was himself a Labour councillor. However, at this General Election, he was a parliamentary candidate, (albeit in an unwinnable seat). He therefore left the organisation of the school election to another teacher who had little interest in it.

Indeed, as if to try to prove a point, a senior prefect was encouraged to stand in the election as a 'Silly' candidate, and what were to be fairly constructive open-air rallies, were turned into a farce with the assembled school being encouraged not just to heckle, but to shout down the candidates.

118

On this, my first outing at the 'hustings', I intended to win and decided to make my own preparations for the day when I was due to address the school.

On the day in question, no one appeared to notice two school 'janitors' moving some electrical equipment onto a fire escape high above the crowd. As the appointed time arrived, the teacher running the show noticed one of the 'janitors' (me!) discarding his overall to reveal a school blazer.

The electrical equipment was a 100 watt pop group amplifier and, perfectly within the rules of the campaign, I proceeded to blast my address to the crowd, completely drowning out the hecklers. I unfortunately also disrupted a meeting being held by the headmaster in his study and a service in a nearby church!

The Rt Hon the Lord Waddington

Leader of The House of Lords and Lord Privy Seal
(MP for Nelson and Colne 1968-74, Clitheroe 1979-83, Ribble Valley
1983-90, Government Chief Whip 1987-89, Home Secretary 1989-90)

In 1964, when I was Conservative candidate for Nelson and Colne, a local vicar told me that there was to be a church service to herald the opening of the campaign and that I was to read the first lesson and Sydney Silverman the second. He gave me his text but when I went home to swot it up I was disappointed to discover that it was a long genealogical table beginning with Abraham begat Isaac and Isaac begat Jacob and thereafter down through the generations.

The service started well and I read my lesson with all the verve and enthusiasm I could command. I returned to my pew well satisfied: but after another psalm it was Sydney Silverman's turn. "Revelations 21," he began, and then with his voice cracking with emotion, "I saw a new Heaven and a new earth."

And I knew I had lost the campaign – before it had even started.

But I had forgotten something which any politician should have remembered. Revelations Chapter 21 is part of the funeral service: four years later Sydney Silverman was under the sod and I was Member of Parliament for Nelson and Colne.

The Rt Hon John Gummer MP

Member for Suffolk Coastal, Minister of Agriculture, Fisheries and Food

(Chairman of the Conservative Party 1983-85)

As an undergraduate at Cambridge, I was canvassing in the 1959 General Election for Sir Hamilton Kerr, who pronounced his name to rhyme with 'far'.

I banged on one door, to be faced with a huge lorry driver who glowered at me from the top step. I said that I was calling on behalf of Sir Hamilton Kerr (car) and I hoped that we could count on his vote.

"Kerr" said the lorry driver, "Kerr, I calls him cur – and I always say, like name like nature."

I put him down as a doubtful!

Sir Robert Rhodes James MP

Member for Cambridge

I have always been a keen believer in stealing my opponents' clothes when appropriate and useful, a practice I commend warmly to all aspiring Conservatives.

The first General Election in which I had a vote was 1955, when I was at Oxford. In those days the political public meeting was an Event, and my friends and I went to the Labour rally in the Town Hall, addressed by, among others, Frank Pakenham (now Lord Longford).

We were resolved to give him a hard time, but, after one of my interventions, Frank looked down with an air of sadness and said, "If our young friend would come here with an open mind instead of an open mouth, he might learn something!"

I was so impressed that I have used the same put-down on several occasions when heckled by Labour or Liberal supporters at public meetings, and thereby gained a totally undeserved reputation for my droll wit.

The Rt Hon the Viscount Whitelaw

(*MP for Penrith and Borders 1955-83, Deputy Leader of the Conservative Party 1975-1991*)

A t the first election which I won at Penrith and the Borders in 1955, a very strange old farmer, and a great character, stood as an Independent, favouring cock fighting and better pay for mole catchers. He went round all the pubs during the election making bets on how many votes he would get. He actually got 300, which was 150 more than he expected. He was therefore collecting money during the end of the count and as soon as he had it, he began to enjoy the proceeds.

Shortly after the announcement, he came up to me and said, "You have stolen all my votes, all my yellow votes." Yellow was, and is of course, the Conservative colour in Cumbria, and he had simply used it as well. "Bundles and bundles of them, you have stolen the lot."

Then he faced up to me, at which he was carried away by two large policemen, and I became a Member of Parliament for the first time.

David Trippier MP

Member for Rossendale and Darwen, Minister for the Environment and the Countryside
(Deputy Chairman of the Conservative Party, 1990)

I was addressing a meeting in the largest public hall in my constituency, which was packed out – with chairs – and only three men and a dog sitting in them.

The Chairman started by introducing me with an attack on the audience, saying:

"If many more of you do not come to these meetings we will *never* get a decent speaker!"

The Chairman seemed to suffer from delusions of adequacy and, despite the fact that he was a well-known Conservative Party supporter, went rattling on. He said:

"When this Government came to power in 1979, this Nation stood on the edge of a precipice, since when we have taken a giant step forward."

List of Contributors

Robert Adley MP, 13
Rupert Allason MP, 101
The Rt Hon Julian Amery
  MP, 107
Sir Thomas Arnold MP, 39
The Rt Hon Kenneth
  Baker MP, 58
Nicholas Baker MP, 22
Tony Baldry MP, 28, 37, 67
The Rt Hon the Lord
  Barber, 31
Vivian Bendall MP, 104
The Rt Hon Sir Frederic
  Bennett, 111
The Lord Bethell MEP, 55
The Rt Hon John Biffen
  MP, 50
Baroness Blatch, 85, 106
The Rt Hon the Lord
  Boardman, 70
The Rt Hon the Lord
  Boyd-Carpenter, 20, 69, 113
Sir Richard Body MP, 87
The Rt Hon Sir Bernard
  Braine MP, 84
Julian Brazier MP, 115
Sydney Chapman MP, 74, 102
Winston S. Churchill MP, 111
The Rt Hon Sir William
  Clark MP, 99
Simon Coombs MP, 85
Patrick Cormack MP, 73

Edwina Currie MP, 30, 87
The Viscount Davidson, 78
Hugh Dykes MP, 54
Lord Elliott of Morpeth, 26
Sir Peter Emery MP, 93
David Evans MP, 68
Barry Field MP, 51
Dudley Fishburn MP, 86
Dame Janet Fookes DBE MP, 35
The Rt Hon the Lord
  Fraser of Carmyllie, 46
Alastair Goodlad MP, 102
Martin Graham, 90
Harry Greenway MP, 61, 116
John Greenway MP, 72
The Rt Hon John
  Gummer MP, 121
The Rt Hon the Lord
  Hailsham of
  Marylebone KG, CH, 29
John Hannam MP, 96
Ken Hargreaves MP, 68, 81
The Rt Hon the Lord
  Havers, 58
Sir Paul Hawkins MP, 96
Jerry Hayes MP, 110
The Rt Hon Edward
  Heath MP, 103, 115
The Rt Hon Michael
  Howard MP, 13
The Rt Hon David Howell
  MP, 41

Michael Jack MP, 89

The Rt Hon the Lord
Jenkin of Roding, 43, 94

The Rt Hon Michael
Jopling MP, 65

Sir Anthony Kershaw, 15, 69

The Lord Kimball, 16

Roger King MP, 86

Greg Knight MP, 18, 25, 54, 118

John Lacy, 37

The Rt Hon Ian Lang MP, 33

John Lee MP, 21, 59

Jim Lester MP, 95

Sir Kenneth Lewis, 71, 75, 80

The Rt Hon Sir Nicholas
Lyell MP, 97

Sir Robert McCrindle
MP, 89

Sir Patrick McNair-Wilson
MP, 105

David Madel MP, 94

Sir Michael Marshall MP, 53

Iain Mills MP, 62, 114

Sir Peter Mills MP, 62, 98, 114

Andrew Mitchell MP, 77

The Rt Hon Sir Peter
Morrison MP, 64

David Mudd MP, 31

Sir Tom Normanton, 20

The Rt Hon Cranley
Onslow MP, 90

The Rt Hon the Baroness
Oppenheim-Barnes, 82

The Rt Hon Cecil
Parkinson MP, 19

James Pawsey MP, 46

Elizabeth Peacock
MP, 18

David Porter MP, 23

Sir Reg Prentice, 78

The Rt Hon the Lord
Renton, 73

Sir Robert Rhodes James
MP, 36, 75, 79, 92, 106, 122

The Rt Hon Sir Wyn
Roberts MP, 17

The Hon Timothy
Sainsbury MP, 44

Jonathan Sayeed MP, 48, 52

Sir Dudley Smith MP, 47

Allan Stewart MP, 56

The Rt Hon Sir Ian
Stewart MP, 92

Sir John Stokes MP, 66

Hugo Summerson MP, 49

Ian Taylor MP, 49, 109

Peter Temple-Morris
MP, 32

Donald Thompson MP, 65

David Trippier MP, 123

Baroness Trumpington. 63, 66

Sir William van
Straubenzee, 45

Peter Viggers MP, 14

The Rt Hon the Lord
Waddington, 120

The Rt Hon John
Wakeham MP, 24

Christine Wall, 40

Kenneth Warren MP, 100

John Watson, 17, 25, 44, 51

Sir John Wheeler MP, 93

The Rt Hon the Viscount
Whitelaw, 61, 109, 117, 122

Nicholas Winterton
MP, 28